Tracy Sahib, Servant of Christ in India

By
Olive G. Tracy

Edited By
R. Franklin Cook

2019-20 NMI
MISSION EDUCATION RESOURCES

Books

TRACY SAHIB,
SERVANT OF CHRIST IN INDIA
by Olive G. Tracy
Edited by R. Franklin Cook

SHIRO KANO
Faithfulness at Any Price
by Alice Spangenberg
Edited by Merritt Nielson

WHAT BEGINS HERE
TRANSFORMS THE WORLD
by Debbie Salter Goodwin

Tracy Sahib, Servant of Christ in India

By
Olive G. Tracy

Edited By
R. Franklin Cook

NAZARENE MISSIONS INTERNATIONAL

First Printing, 1954
Second Printing, 1990, revised and condensed by Helen Temple
Third Printing, 2018, revised and updated by R. Franklin Cook

ISBN 978-0-8341-3765-3

Printed in the United States of America

Cover design: Darryl Bennett
Cover photo: Nazarene Archives
Interior design: Darryl Bennett

Table of Contents

Introductory Editor's Note 6

Prelude: A Splendid Subcontinent 9

Olive's Introduction 15

Chapter 1
Now Therefore Go 17

Chapter 2
As for Me and My House, We Will Serve the Lord 23

Chapter 3
Thou Shalt Be like a Watered Garden 31

Chapter 4
It Was Not You That Sent Me Hither, but God 39

Chapter 5
In Earing Time and in Harvest Thou Shalt Rest 51

Chapter 6
Behold, I Have Set the Land Before You 63

Chapter 7
Ye Shall Sow the Land 71

Chapter 8
His Word Was in Mine Heart as a Burning Fire 87

Chapter 9
Mine Eyes Shall Be upon the Faithful of the Land 101

Chapter 10
The Voice of Rejoicing and Salvation 115

Postlude : A Splendid Sacrifice 123

A Growing Church 131

Act On It 135

Introductory Editor's Note:

Dr. R. Franklin Cook has done a masterful job of bringing *Tracy Sahib of India*[1] up to date. Cook's grandparents, Rev. Frank and Ruby Blackman, arrived as missionaries in the northeast sector of the Indian subcontinent, working in Kishorganj, now in Bangladesh. Frank Blackman died of smallpox as a result of serving communion to a sailor in Calcutta in 1925. The Blackman's daughter, Orpha returned to the United States, and eventually married Ralph Cook. They returned to India in 1935, missionaries in Buldana, Maharashtra, with Franklin, then only ten months old. Franklin Cook grew up in India, and though he left at aged 16, India remained a formative influence on his life. In 1989, Cook was named regional director of the Eurasia Region, which happily included the Indian subcontinent. His historical perspective, keen insight, and love for India helped the church there to grow and mature. No one is better suited to revise this book than he.

---

[1] Tracy Sahib of India was the original title Olive Tracy gave to the book about her father and his missionary work in India. Sahib is a word that comes from the Arabic, meaning "friend."

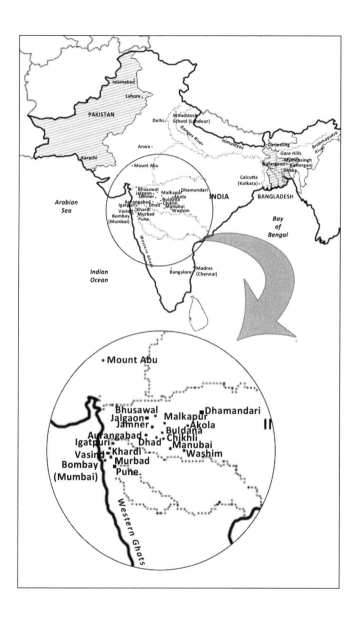

Prelude: A Splendid Subcontinent

"Oh, East is East and West is West
and never the twain shall meet,
Till Earth and Sky stand presently at
God's great Judgement Seat."
Rudyard Kipling

John Kenneth Galbraith, esteemed past USA ambassador to India, often described India as "functioning anarchy."

A more apt description would be hard to find. A first-time visitor will be overwhelmed by the sheer chaos of the place. There seems no order, no system, no pattern. Every truck, car, and three-wheeler finds its own way through traffic. Roads accommodate vehicular traffic and stray dogs and cows. At the side of every road are merchants—India is made up of entrepreneurial merchants by the millions. Signboards in a variety of languages, including the uniquely Indian English language, can be seen everywhere. One might hear the call to prayer of the Muslim, or the clanging bells of the Hindu temple. And the horns, always the horns, which every driver feels compelled to honk non-stop. It is anarchy.

But it is functional. I often told first time visitors to India, usually sitting terrified in the back of a taxi, to relax.

"There really is a system, and it works." And it does. One of the miracles of India is that a nation made up of amazing variety, almost beyond calculation, functions. It is "functional anarchy."

Rudyard Kipling was perhaps the best-known writer of his generation, late 19th and early 20th century. His father had worked in India as a civil servant for almost 30 years, and Rudyard spent the first 6 years of his life there during the height of colonial rule by Britain. Later in life, Rudyard spent another 6 years living and working in India. The impact of the culture was so profound in his life that it affected all his later writing. He wrote such world-class bestsellers as Kim and The Jungle Book. For these and many other works, Kipling was awarded the Nobel Prize for literature in 1907.

One memorable observation Rudyard Kipling made this: "the first condition of understanding a foreign country is to smell it." As amusing as this may seem, it is true. And India presents any visitor with a suffocating array of smells. The dust, curries and spices, the fragrance of Ganges Primrose, Lotus, Jasmine, Hibiscus and the exotic Frangipanis. Even body odor in India has a unique pungency. No place on earth can present the variety of smells that India can present.

It is interesting to note that the life of Rudyard Kipling in the span of history is very close to that of the subject of this book, L. S. Tracy. Therefore, the observations made by Kipling about India were those accurately reflected by Tracy as he trekked across the land beginning in 1903.

Frequently I reminded visitors that whatever preconception of India they had, they were almost sure to be wrong.

Many visitors expect universal poverty. But India has incredible wealth. Many expect dust and desert. But India has the most awesome and highest mountains in the world. And lush tropical fields of rice and coconuts. Many expect oxcarts and buffaloes, but India has some of the most incredible high tech industries in the world. Some think of hot curry, but India has hundreds, perhaps thousands, of varieties of food with regional specialities. Menus often break down food to south or north India cuisine. Yes, almost every preconception is wrong in one way or another.

India is a land of astronomical numbers. Packed in to a land mass a third the size of the United States at a ratio of 1,180 persons per square mile are currently almost 1.4 billion people, 18% of the world's population. And if you take "pre-partition"[2] India (including Pakistan and Bangladesh) you increase the population size to approximately 1.8 billion persons. The population growth projection is that today's India will exceed China in population by the year 2050.[3]

Almost any other number cited in the Indian context is large. Whether it is the volume of trash or the Indian diaspora around the world. Considering the median age in India today is 27, and what is considered the "middle class"

---

[2] Partition refers to the desperate act of Britain to solve communal and religions violence in India by dividing the land between predominantly Muslim and Hindu areas, resulting in the 1947 partitioning of the country into what was Pakistan and Bangladesh. The resulting migration is considered the largest in history with millions uprooted and many killed.

[3] There are a number of organizations who provide demographic data, including agencies of the United Nations. These numbers are equivalent citations from several sources.

of new, urban, educated consumers, is about 400,000,000 India is a force in the world to be reckoned with.

India has the largest number of ethnic groups in the world. India has 18 recognized languages (not including English, which is de facto the *lingua franca*[4] of the country), plus hundreds of dialects. India has a wide range of political parties and attitudes, from Hindu nationalism to the secularism of its constitution.

India is a photographer's paradise. The beauty of its children, the glow in their eyes, the dazzling gold and color of women's garb the sari, the uniqueness of the flowing dhoti worn by many farmers, designer jeans worn by urban youth, the jewelry in one of the most gold and silver rich nations on earth, the highest number of motion pictures produced by any country on earth of what is commonly called Bollywood, the hundreds of television channels, the prolific production of poetry and music, the complexity of national media outlets in a nation of many languages. All of this is the Splendor of the Sub Continent.

The world in to which Leighton Tracy stepped as a young, single missionary, in 1903, was India. The clarion call of the Gospel compelled many young to devote their lives to China, Africa, and India (the primary "targets" for missionaries in the 19th century). They brought with them passion, tenacity, and sacrifice. They gave their lives, endured opposition, hardship, deprivation, and usually an abject lack of resources.

---

[4]   *lingua franca* is defined as a language that is adopted as a common language between speakers whose native languages are different.

In 1954 Ms. Olive Tracy, daughter of L. S. Tracy, was asked to write her memories of her dad. She used as a primary source her mother Gertrude, whose recollections were colored by time and experience. Olive herself had carved out a significant career as a corporate executive for CBS (Columbia Broadcasting System), and applied her skills to the text you find here. The love for her father is obvious. We have chosen to leave, for the most part, the text as Olive wrote it. You may find the phrases dated and stilted—they came out of their time and context.

But the message is clear. Whatever missionary life is today, and whatever the church is today, it is built on the blood of martyrs and the philosophy of these indomitable pioneers. The India Tracy entered in 1903 (with his career lasting for the next 30 years) was at the height of the colonial era when India (including Pakistan and Bangladesh) was the "Crown of the Jewel of the Empire." In fact, the title of British Monarch's was Name followed by the words "by the Grace of God, of Great Britain, Ireland and the British Dominions beyond the Seas, King, Defender of the Faith, Emperor of India." So, Tracy entered an India as part of the British Empire and this can be observed in several references in the text.

The Protestant denominations in India devised a system called *comity*, by which geographical areas were assigned to each group. Thus, the three areas the Church of the Nazarene worked in (East, Central, and West) had been assigned under the comity system. The purpose, of course, was to reduce confusion and competition, but the result was such strange mixes as Indians belonging to the Church of Scotland, or Lutherans, or Methodists, according to geography rather than theology or choice. If you were Christian, you were this or that.

The times were different but the cause the same. That is, bringing the peace and message of Jesus to those who were living in spiritual darkness in one of the most religious nations on earth. And establishing the indigenous church which could carry on the task of evangelism. These pioneering missionaries did the best they could with the knowledge, the context, and the resources they had at their disposal.

Read with understanding and compassion and let your eyes be opened by the life and work of Tracy, servant of Christ in India.

—R. FRANKLIN COOK

Olive's Introduction

"I don't quite know how to do it," I said to my mother as we sat talking over the assignment to create this book. "The commission has asked for an account of Dad's life and labors in India. But there are so many others besides him— all the missionaries of his day and later, the Indian church, Dad's associates from other missions. And the family—you and Grandma and Martha and Phil, and I suppose I'm in it too. It's like the big banyan tree that grows in Buldana and spreads over Stone Hall. The whole tree is India, the mission field, the work done. All those who have helped in the work are the trunks and aerial roots that go down and spread out farther and farther. How can I possibly tell it all?"

"I don't think you can include it all," Mom said. "Our own little 'trunk of the great tree' is about the best you can do."

And so here it is—just our small part of this great work, with Dad (Tracy Sahib, as the Indians called him) dominating and directing this little share in the great land that is India.

—OLIVE TRACY

Rev. Leighton S. Tracy

15

(L to R) Dr. Williams, Dr. Goodwin, Leighton Tracy, Gertrude P. Tracy

The Tracy Family

Chapter 1

Now Therefore Go

Exodus 4:12

Moses and Dad were kindred spirits. There was a bond that knit them together from the time that Dad first began to give Moses' arguments to the Lord, and the Lord repeated to him the same answers He had given Moses.

"Who am I, that I should go … ?" Dad contended, quoting Exod. 3:11. The Lord would not consider his various reasonings. He simply led Dad's eyes down the page to the next verse. "Certainly, I will be with thee," the promise fairly shouted at Dad from the page.

"But—but—" stammered Dad, jumping to the fourth chapter for another crutch. "'I am not eloquent … I am slow of speech, and of a slow tongue'" (v. 10).

There, that did it. It was true. In fact, there was a distinct hesitation, a little impediment in his speech.

Yet the call kept coming. And God added, "You will proclaim My gospel more in another tongue than in your good Canadian English."

I have heard Dad tell this story many times. Not only did his tongue grasp the intricacies of another language, so that he spoke fluent Marathi and understood Bengali, Hindustani, and a bit of Sanskrit, but he so identified with the people that he thought and felt much as they did.

On a Sunday morning when Dad was 10 years old, he first met God in a little Reformed Baptist church in Hartland, N.B. He was 16 when he sought and found the experience of a clean heart at a New Brunswick, Canada camp meeting.

Work was difficult to find in those years. Dad accepted the invitation of a Christian man to go to Haverhill, Mass., to work. Along the Merrimack River, in Grandview Park, a short streetcar ride from Haverhill, a new camp meeting was organizing. Dad helped build a dormitory, dining hall, and tabernacle. He attended the services several times.

Moses and Dad were kindred spirits. There was a bond that knit them together...

In August 1901 Dad wrote to his mother:

"Dear Mother, I attended the camp meeting the last three days. Since I have been there, the Lord has changed my life, upset all my plans, and given me new ones.

"One day Mrs. H. F. Reynolds spoke about the school at Saratoga Springs, N.Y., and immediately there was a desire created in me to go there. I told the Lord that if He wanted me to preach and would make a way for me to get an education, to make it so plain that I could not mistake it. The president of the school came to camp on Saturday. The Lord said, 'You ought to go to that school.'

"But I said, 'Lord, I haven't any money.'

"Then the question came, 'Will you go if I will open the way?'

"I said, 'Yes, Lord, if You will open the way, and go with me, and make it so plain that I cannot mistake it, I will go.'

"After the service, I asked some of the people to stay with me, and we would pray over it. I was so broken up that I could not speak. The Holy Ghost was there in mighty power. After a while I calmed down and told God all about it.

"While I was praying, the people around me began to subscribe money for my education. When I was through, $110 was pledged; and at the same time, I got the clear witness that God wanted me to go. Glory to God!

"One year's study would cost $125, including board, washing, tuition, carpeted room, fuel, light, use of library, reading room, and so on. So, I am $15.00 short. That does not include my fare there, books about $7.00, or clothing. I will have to furnish my own towels, napkins, broom, dustpan, one bedspread, one comforter blanket, three sheets, two pairs of pillowcases, one knife and fork, one small and large spoon in case of sickness.

"Maybe you think I am rash in going there, but it is not me, it is God. I did not choose the calling, but He called me, and I *dare* not disobey.

"I start for Saratoga Springs next Wednesday, the 10th of September, and am believing God for the money. I am not going to ask you if I can go. God has called me beyond a doubt, and I have no right to ask you (I say it reverently), but I do ask you and the people to help me with your prayers and money, if you can."

In his letters to his mother that first year, Dad wrote not only of his hopes and aspirations but also of the privations of the students, the cold rooms, the oatmeal and hominy for breakfast, the inevitable potatoes and beef and pudding for dinner. He wondered if he should take piano lessons; they cost an extra 25 cents a lesson. My mother tells me that he did finally take a few, but he never learned anything much; it just wasn't in him. She should know— she was his teacher.

Dad wrote his mother how his old brown trousers were being patched too often, but that Mother Perry, with quick, experienced fingers and brown silk, had manipulated his sacrificed vest into a work of art, and hardly anyone ever guessed how his trousers became so miraculously durable. Mother Perry was dean, nurse, counselor, housekeeper, and "mother" to all lonely boys and girls away from home.

That first year spent in the little institute was a hard one. Dad worked there through the summer when the summer guests were occupying the building. He worked long hours; and one day they found him in the chapel where his cot was, on his knees praying, but sound asleep.

That winter in Saratoga Springs Dad was down in the old boiler room one day where he stoked the school's coal furnaces. He was praying alone, refreshing his consecration and laying his entire future in the hands of his God. In return, he received an overwhelming blessing. His life stretched out ahead glowing with promise.

And then, in a remarkably poignant chapel service, another very special meeting with God came!

In a letter to his mother dated January 15, 1902, he wrote, "I am now going to tell you something that might surprise you. Last Friday morning in chapel, God gave me a clear, definite call to India.[5] I dropped to my knees to know if it was God's voice, and it came so plainly to me that the devil cannot beat it out of me. I felt the power of the Holy Ghost as never before. God wants me thoroughly prepared, so I will stay here the seven years, I expect, then give my life to the mission field."

The call! There was no coercion in it, no bribe of glitter and romance or lure of the tropics. Outlined on the curtaining fog of the future was only one thing—the one thing that was often to stand alone against idolatrous darkness in the years ahead —*the call*, clear, brilliantly etched, and haloed with the promises, "Now therefore go, and I will be with thy mouth, and teach thee what thou shalt say" (Exod. 4:12), and "Certainly I will be with thee" (3:12).

---

[5] During and 19th and early 20th centuries, it was quite common for those called of God to sense a specific country or area of calling. Typically, these were either China, Africa, or India. In these times (now), God's call tends to be to a certain vocation or skill set, rather than to a geographical location.

Chapter 2

As for Me and My House, We Will Serve the Lord

Joshua 24:15

It may well have been God's original plan that Leighton Tracy stay in school the prescribed seven years of preparation to fit him for his mission work. But the school did not last that long; there was disruption in its ranks. Some of the key personnel wished to become independent; others wished to remain with the General Pentecostal Board.[6] Those choosing to stay with the Board left Saratoga Springs and relocated in North Scituate, R.I., calling themselves the Pentecostal Collegiate Institute. With this group went my grandmother, "Mother" Ella Winslow Perry, and her son and daughter, Ernest and Gertrude, both teachers. They, with others, readied the buildings in the summer and fall of

---

[6] The word 'Pentecostal' was often used to identify institutions or organizations associated with holiness or other expressions of the "Spirit-led life". In fact, the Church of the Nazarene was first named "The Pentecostal Church of the Nazarene". The word "Pentecostal" became associated with speaking in tongues or ecstatic utterances", and the Church of the Nazarene rejected this practice. The word "Pentecostal" was dropped from the name in 1919.

1902. Armed with pails and mops and wallpaper and brushes and paint, they polished the old rooms of the abandoned normal school they had purchased, fixed the fireplaces, oriented the classrooms, cooked the first meals, and opened the doors to the few students who enrolled.

Young Leighton Tracy was not one of them. Sick at heart and disgusted at the happenings in Saratoga Springs, he took his old brass cornet and joined a group called the Pentecostal Bands. For a few months, he traveled with one of these bands holding evangelistic meetings. Then his need of preparation for his lifework pressed down on him again, and in the winter of 1904 he went to North Scituate and renewed his studies.

During that same season, Martyn D. Wood and his wife, Anna, visited the campus of Pentecostal Collegiate Institute. They had come from India to raise money and recruit personnel to help in their work. They had gone to India 11 years before, supported by the Christian and Missionary Alliance, had changed church affiliations a time or two since, and were presently working under the newly formed Association of Pentecostal Churches of America, led by H. F. Reynolds.

M. D. Wood had a small mission, first in Igatpuri (EE-guht-poo-ree), near Bombay[7], and then in Buldana (bull- DAWN-uh), in Berar Province of central India. On its eight acres was an orphanage for victims of the famine of 1897, along with three bungalows, and they hoped to build a hospital. Helpers were badly needed.

_____
[7] Bombay has been renamed Mumbai, in Maharashtra State, on the western side of the sub-Continent.

It was a challenge! In the institute, four felt pressed to go with others Wood had recruited: Leighton Tracy, a student; Julia Gibson of Saratoga Springs, who had just graduated; Gertrude Perry, teacher of English; and Mother Perry, dean of women, general housekeeper, and practical nurse.

In November 1902, Ernest Perry, brother of Gertrude, had drowned in a canoe accident. The small insurance received after his death provided the way for Mother Perry and Gertrude to join the group going to India. Mother Perry paid her own and her daughter's fare and deposited with the association another $200 to guarantee her fare home if her health should fail within two years.

Two months before the party was scheduled to sail, word came from India that things were not going well there.

Pushing out from the North German Lloyd pier in New York on July 2, 1904, the prospective missionaries agreed that it was a beautiful day. They had farewelled from the Utica Avenue Pentecostal Church in Brooklyn the night before. Now they stood along the railing of the ship, waving handkerchiefs to loved ones and friends gathered in a knot at the end of the wharf. Dad picked up his cornet and put it to his lips. Across the widening water, he played his theme song, "Where Jesus Is, Tis Heaven There."

The missionaries took another look at the city behind them that represented home, cried a little as the Statue of Liberty slid by, wiped their eyes, and then went to the bow and looked off through the Narrows and out to sea. There was scarcely a ripple on the ocean. They watched the water turn from green to the blue-green of the continental shelf, and from blue to purple, and finally to the purple-black of the deeps, mottled and marbled with white by the wake of the twisting screws.

In Genoa, Italy they transferred to the Italian liner *Balduiono*. Piles of baggage to be transferred, seven women and three children to be looked after, and only two men to do the heavy lifting. It was a thrilling adventure, the three youngest adults told each other—Julia Gibson, Gertrude Perry, and Leighton Tracy. They stayed up late and watched the moon spring full-grown out of the jeweled Mediterranean, made up silly poems about it and one another, and laughed and were happy.

They shopped in Genoa, walked in the ruins of Pompeii, and bought their thick cork helmets[8] in Aden.

They should have met the full force of the monsoon rain in the Indian Ocean, but there was only light rain. Only a third of the rain needed to feed India fell that monsoon season. The new missionaries did not realize the full significance of this until later.

It was August 5, 1904, and this was India. Everything wore a halo of beauty. There was the island that was Bombay, and their ship rattled out its anchors in the channel because it was low tide. From the pier came rowboat ferries with M. D. Wood aboard one of them. They all bobbed ashore in the little shell. There were mountains of baggage to sort. They

---

[8] "Thick cork helmets" refers to what were called "pith helmets". Those from the West were expected to wear them as protection from the severity of tropical sun. Thus, the unique appearance in old photographs of missionaries (or British soldiers-officers).

counted and checked and found that one of the Perry trunks was missing. It was four months before the Perrys could have their new shoes and bolts of cloth for new dresses.

Two days of shopping ended when they boarded the train at seven in the evening for a night journey inland. They found five narrow benches for seven women and three children. The previous inhabitants crawled in and out freely.

All night long they wound and swayed over the steep mountain grades of the Western Ghats (ghawts). Tilting, sliding, cramped, and aching, they "slept" the night out. Often there was a screech of brakes as the train catapulted to a sudden stop. Through the window slats the missionaries saw the hurrying coolies[9] on the platform, and then the smiles and hellos of friends of the Woods who had come to welcome them back to India. There were introductions, quick bits of news thrown back and forth, lunches passed in through opened window or door—sandwiches, boiled eggs, late mangoes—then a jolt, grinding wheels, and good-bye voices fading in the distance.

At six in the morning they changed trains at Bhusawal (bhoo-SAW-wuhl) and two hours later arrived on the little platform at Malkapur (MUHL-kuh-poo-er), the station for the Buldana mission. Lunches given during the night provided breakfast. Tongas and carts were waiting. A tonga is a two-wheeled vehicle drawn by a pair of bullocks or ponies. It has good covering against the heat of the sun and, though

---

9   In the context of India, this term is used to refer to someone who assists travelers with heavy parcels and baggage at ports and stations.

not luxurious, does have springs and cushions. Each holds four people: two facing forward and two facing back.

The mail tongas[10] were the fastest, changing ponies every 7 to 10 miles. The Wood family took the mail tonga, the others climbed into the mission tonga, and the three young people went in the mission cart.

The carts of India are a wonder. They have developed little since the dim mists of humankind's earliest history when some progressive inventor first found or made a round disc and rolled it along the ground, calling it a wheel. Joining two with an axle, adding a platform and a light railing, a tongue with a seat for the driver, and two humpbacked bullocks, and the freight of this great subcontinent jogs along its roads. In spite of aircraft, railroads, paved highways, cars, and buses, the bullock cart is still there[11], reliable, and available to everyone who has the time.

The young people had the time. They left Malkapur around nine in the morning and reached Buldana about six that evening. And in that 28 miles they learned a little of India and a lot about oxcarts.

The mission cart had no seats. There were two thin cotton pillows and one cushion with a few weak springs.

---

[10] A tonga is a cart, typically covered by a canopy, pulled by a single horse. Under the British system, getting the mail through as quickly as possible was a priority, so it tended to be transported by 'tongas'.

[11] Those visiting India today will notice heavy motorized traffic. Bullock carts are mostly seen in rural or remote areas of the country. However, much of the danger that exists on rural roads in India is due to the presence of bullock carts competing for the same road as overloaded transport trucks or speeding private vehicles. It can be quite chaotic.

Whenever the driver could frighten the oxen into a sudden run, the girls screamed and bounced, and the clumsy pith hats went bounding and flopping. Hairpins flew all over the cart floor to get lost in the baggage and scattered on the road. And the driver would look back and grin.

The missionaries gazed at the beauty of the flowering trees and hedges, the fields of cotton and grain and newly green jungle. It came to them that scattered all through were little gray mud huts and temples and idols and people. There were also fever and cholera and plague and leprosy and evil of every kind. Their young hearts yearned with a hot flame of love for the Master, and as they jogged along, they prayed for these people.

And they sang, believing every word:

Farther on the way grows brighter;
Count the milestones one by one:
Jesus will forsake me never,
It is better farther on.

Presently the cart crossed the Vishwaganga (VEESH-wuh-GUHN-guh) River and began to climb up, up to the 2,190-foot level of the great tableland of central India, on the north edge of which is the town of Buldana (bull-DAWN-uh). And then they were at the mission. The iron-barred gate, set in the corrugated tin of the compound fence, swung open; Elmer Burgess, who had gone to India earlier, waved them welcome. The orphan children, clapping and shouting, lined the driveway. As the missionaries climbed out of the cart stiffly, two little girls came, shy and smiling, bringing flowers with which all India welcomes her guests and her sons.

Leighton Tracy looked around, stretched his long, cramped legs, and thanked God that this was to be his land, his work, his life. At that moment, the call was a living thing, clear and glowing. He was eight days from his 22nd birthday.

Chapter 3

Thou Shalt Be like
a Watered Garden
Isaiah 58:11

Buldana was the chief town of the district. Even in 1901 it had 4,173 citizens. More than 3,000 were Hindus; about 800 were Muslims; and there were 114 Christians.[12] The courthouse and the jail were across the road from the mission. There were rows and rows of little gray houses and shops with grass growing from the flat roofs.

Not far from the mission was a caravansary.[13] One of the caravan routes led past our front gate. I remember how we would hear the padding of the soft-footed camels, cadently measured in the hollow clinking of crude, tinny bells as the great, laden beasts swung along.

---

[12] In the 2011 Census, Buldana City had 67,431 population though the surrounding district has more than 2.5 million populations. In the city, Hindus were 59%, Muslims, 24%, and Christians categorized as "other".

[13] A caravansary is an inn on a caravan route. A word used more often in the Middle East as a resting place on the caravan routes. OR…an overnight guest house.

Buldana had a government hospital for the Indian people. My sister, Martha, and I were born in Stone Hall on the mission, however, and the doctor of the town's hospital came and attended our arrivals. Since little girl babies are not considered very important in India, the clerk in the courthouse who made out our birth certificates neglected to write in our names. In consequence both Martha and I have had trouble proving legally that we were born.

I remember the tangled pattern of the bazaar: heavy with musk and sandalwood blended with strings of drying fish, the smell of sweet hay and dung-fire smoke, the tipped-up carts and hot animals, battered iron weights placed in one pan of the brass balances with grain piled in the other, the bangle merchant who forced the colorful glass bracelets over tight knuckles, stacks of shining brassware, six-armed idols in rows, and the indescribably sharp, acrid scent of cloth that stings the nostrils.

Buldana had post and telegraph offices, a hotel, a cemetery, government schools for girls and boys, a high school, and a water system with six tanks that distributed through six-inch pipes to 53 private connections and 30 standposts, with a daily authorized supply of 40,000 gallons for 24 hours.

One of these standpipes was on the mission compound. The water ran into two wooden tubs connected by a pipe and green with a slippery growth. The overflow slopped into an open sluice and ran off into the garden. We did not drink this water until it was thoroughly boiled. Then it went into large, covered earthenware jars that stood on the coolest spot of the veranda of Stone Hall ready for anyone who wanted a drink. A battered and chipped enamel dipper hung on the side of the rack that held the jars, and the tepid, lukewarm, tasteless liquid was all I knew as drinking water. The only time it tasted good was in the cold season when the wind blew around the jars at night.

The average rainfall for Buldana was nearly 32 inches. But in 1904 the rains had not come. By fall it was evident that there would be a water famine. It was ruled that the town water flow to the mission was to be stopped on September 15. It was also ruled that the dairy of 23 buffalo and the mission school for boys were to be moved outside the municipality.

The dairy had been started to give employment to Christians. As Hindus became Christians, their villages cast them out. They had nowhere to go and no way to earn a living. Dad was the farm boy of the mission group. He was assigned to take charge of the dairy.

When the evacuation edict was given to M. D. Wood, the mission went to prayer. They gathered on the veranda of the Woods' home. Wood led, the missionaries and teachers prayed, and then some of the older schoolchildren prayed. Rain; we must have rain, O God. ... Rain. ... The tanks are nearly empty. ... Rain. ... O Lord, answer by sending rain." Prayer rose on prayer, petition lifted on petition. With hands raised together, they piled high an altar of prayer like Elijah. And when at last they went out into the night to look for their answer, two small clouds were running before the heat lightning against the southern stars, and a light breath of thunder rolled out of the dark. Before morning it was pouring rain. For six days and nights it swept over them, wave on wave, until their shouts of joy turned to cries of "Enough, Lord, enough." And when the sun came again, a glad procession went down to the big tank to watch the splashing overflow.

The town water supply was not cut off, but the mission still needed land for the dairy. About a mile and a half from the mission, just outside the city line, was a 23-acre piece of land. It had soil for farming and grazing land, and two good springs at the lower end. With much bargaining—for all India loves to bargain—they settled on a price agreeable to all. Then the owners showed their ragged clothes, probably donned for the occasion, and asked for a coat for a present. Some old coats were found and given to them. In addition, the missionaries gave them an old toothless buffalo. Thus, the bargain was sealed.

This farm was called Dhamandari (DHAWM-uhl-dairy).[14] The Dhamandari is a snake. If the land was named for a snake, it would better have been called Naga-land, the missionaries said, for the cobra, *nag*, abounds there.

Dad was a good one to send to the farm. He could take anything apart and put it together again.

He seldom made things just for our personal enjoyment, but we understood that it was because there wasn't time for us. "The work" was always first. Any piece of machinery or

---

[14] The Dhamandari farm is still owned by the church, but is now surrounded by the growing city of Buldana. In one of the buildings meets a thriving local Church of the Nazarene.

tool came alive in his hands. He made a pair of pliers from two broken ones. He fixed a shaving brush, extending its life for several years. Once, when he couldn't get leather to fix his shoes, he put tin soles on them. A big, old-fashioned music box stood in Stone Hall ever since I could remember. It was broken; but when Dad had a few minutes one day, it seemed he only looked at it, and it began playing "Lead, Kindly Light" again, sweet and tinkly.

Clever mechanical magic was all well and good, but nothing can be done without the right tools, and there were no tools at all in the mission when Dad first went there.

"We can't build a farm and a dairy and a mission without tools," Dad said, and promptly made his needs known. There arrived with the next missionary's baggage hammers, a large pipe wrench, saws, braces and bits, pliers, an auger, chisels, hatchets, files, screwdrivers, clamps, spirit levels, planes, mallets, compasses, dividers, rules, awls, drills, dies, nuts and bolts, iron, leather, and woodworking tools; and some child put in his little saw and toy square.

But on the farm, they had to build some kind of shelter before the wonderful tools arrived. They built a small, round, one-room structure of bamboo matting with a grass roof. It served as Dad's house, the dairy milkhouse, and mission storeroom. Dad moved there two days after Christmas, 1904.

Tentlike sheds with grass roofs were built to house the orphan boys. The buffalo were tethered in the open, circled with a thorn hedge to discourage prowlers. It was wild and lonely there. Jackals, wolves, and bands of monkeys were constantly about.

On December 31, 1904, they dedicated the school for the boys. Julia Gibson walked the mile and a half out and back from Buldana for nearly a year to teach English to the boys.

In the meantime, Mother Perry and her daughter, Gertrude, and Priscilla Hitchens were helping in the girls' school, sewing and teaching. The Davidsons were secretary and treasurer, Mrs. Wood and Mrs. Barnes did medical work, and Miss Sprague and Elmer Burgess helped M. D. Wood in village evangelism.

Early in 1905 the Perrys were moved to Chikhli, 14 miles to the south. They started a small school of about half a dozen boys on a veranda. They held meetings in their home; heads popped in and out of the windows, but few came inside.

Then the wife of a prominent Muslim merchant pricked her finger. It became infected, and she was in great pain. The infection was far advanced when the Muslim husband came asking help. Mother Perry looked at the swollen hand and hurried home to make a poultice. Every day Mother Perry applied new poultices. She prayed fervently for the woman. And a miracle came to pass. For days, the woman was in agony; then slowly there was a shade of improvement noticed each day until the finger was well. The reputation of the mission and of the Christian *mem-sahibs* (mem-SAW-heebs) rose, and Chikhli slowly opened its door to them.

In September, the Perrys went back to Buldana, and Julia Gibson and Priscilla Hitchens moved to Chikhli, taking the girls' school with them.

During the next year three of the missionaries had to return home, leaving nine workers.

On the threshold of the new year stood Gertrude Perry and Leighton Tracy. Or rather, they sat on the back seat of the mission tonga that December 31, 1904, as Mrs. Wood and the driver in front urged the oxen back home from a village medical call. It didn't take too much jolting on the rough road for Leighton Tracy's big pith helmet to happen to slide across the edge of his lap in such a way that it covered Gertrude Perry's hand. It wasn't exactly strange that night when Leighton asked Gertrude to walk with him out to the compound gate. "Walking out" was frowned upon in the mission. Such things were not done in India. Such serious things as marriage must be arranged through parents or relatives or impartial agents.

Bowing to prevalent custom for the sake of reputation, the younger missionaries had been forbidden to "walk out" together. The command added urgency to his purpose. Leighton Tracy did not wait for another opportunity to sneak away to the iron gateway. That one forbidden night, under the benevolent, polished copper moon, he asked. And though her answer shyly put him off, the twinkling Southern Cross witnessed that her heart was nodding yes.

They were married in September 1905 and went to live at the Dhamandari farm.

"What do you remember most clearly?" I asked my mother casually.

"The rats." She laughed. "The boldness of the huge beasts not waiting for night, but almost tripping us as we worked during the day. They actually chewed off a corner of a glass bottle. And the bedbugs! We soaked rags in kerosene and wrapped them around the legs of the furniture to try to control them. Not until we whitewashed walls, ceiling, and floor of each room did we get rid of them."

Chapter 4

It Was Not You That Sent Me Hither, but God
Genesis 45:8

The great revival in Wales in 1905 lighted fires all over the world. It jumped into India and spread through all evangelistic channels. It blazed in Buldana's two Christian communities, the Christian and Missionary Alliance and our own school. It left a group of young Indian men and women in our school, zealous, with hearts aflame, preparing to spread the gospel of Jesus Christ in this section of their country. Our mission stood on the edge of great expansion.

Instead there came such a staggering blow that at home it was seriously proposed that the India field be closed.

Calling themselves the "seniors" because they had been in India before, M. D. Wood, Mrs. Wood, and Miss Lillian Sprague proposed independence of any governing board or committee with headquarters on another continent.

A few weeks previous the Missionary Committee at home, headed by Rev. H. F. Reynolds, had appointed three of the missionaries to make final and important decisions for the India mission. The three appointed were M. D. Wood, Lillian Sprague, and L. S. Tracy. But this arrangement was not pleasing to M. D. Wood. It led to the sending of a letter to the Missionary Committee dated November 8, 1905, and bearing the signatures of the three "seniors."[15]

The letter told of urgent calls received by the Woods and Miss Sprague to accept grandiose positions with another mission. "If accepted," Wood wrote, "the Pentecostal Mission would be left rather desolate. The workers who would not accompany us are, in our judgment, thoroughly unqualified in spiritual power, experience, and training to take up duties that now fall on us. If in order to gain your prayers and support, we must be ruled and regulated by you, then we bid you farewell and seek perfect freedom in other fields."

The letter continued, indicating that if they accepted his proposal to be the one head making all decisions, he must have "perfect harmony" from the missionaries; and if this was not so, some would be asked to resign.

A later letter spelled out Wood's demands: no salaries for workers; a general fund providing for food, washing, and a home; and $6.50 a month for expenses.

The five "junior" missionaries, knowing a little of what was going on, sent a letter of their own to the Missionary Committee, declaring faith in the home board and a desire to continue under their leadership.

---

[15] Enshrined in the "Missionary Policy" governing the work of missionaries during this era was the concept of "junior missionary". The first two years in a missionary career, one was a junior with no voting privileges; one was not expected to speak. It was a time of learning the cultures, listening and language acquisition.

There was no airmail service in those days, of course, and cablegrams were too expensive. It took more than two months for the letters to travel and the committee to call an emergency meeting on December 21. In mid-January, their answer was received in Buldana in a letter addressed to L. S. Tracy, with an enclosed letter to be delivered to M. D. Wood. The two nearly identical letters contained the committee's acceptance of the resignation of the three "seniors," their salaries to February 1, and the appointment of L. S. Tracy as superintendent of the mission.

While waiting for the committee's answer, the Tracys were brought in from the farm, and the Woods, Miss Sprague, and Mrs. Barnes moved out there. The girls' school was brought from Chikhli to the farm, but Miss Gibson and Miss Hitchens were left in Chikhli to do evangelistic work. Early in February, about 10 days after the Tracys delivered the letter from the Missionary Committee, they awoke one morning to find a tin box on the veranda of Stone Hall. In it were papers for the Buldana and Chikhli properties—and about 75 cents in Indian money. There was a farewell note explaining that this was all that was left after paying bills.

The Tracys hurried out to the farm. There were no missionaries, no teachers, no school children, no buffalo or dairy. Except for one local preacher, all other personnel and movable property were gone. The Tracys fell to their knees, stunned and scarcely able to pray. Out of the shock and chaos, God's call came again, clear and certain. Go home and admit failure? No! Go on, somehow, with the help of God!

The days following this tragic event were hazy with disbelief. The Tracys contacted the two ladies in Chikhli, cabled the Missionary Committee at home, and had endless conferences.

"Missions in their beginning days," stated Dad, pragmatically, "are apt to be haphazard. They may be opened prematurely; untried missionaries sent out; finances be spasmodic in coming. There is need of far vision, careful economic planning, sound policy, and good business sense. We have no schools, no preachers or workers, so the educational program, the dairying, and other industries are impossible. As I see it, all that is left to do right now is evangelize and get to the people. We can come within 10 feet of the heathen and not reach them, and be just as guilty as if we had stayed at home 10,000 miles away. Evangelize first and educate later when we can first things first!"[16]

Touring was being done by other missions in different parts of India. Dad was quick to see the possibilities of this method of going directly to the people.

Touring is going out for a time to live right in the villages. In the cool of the year, toward the end of November after the rains are over and the weather becomes pleasant, the missionaries pack up their tents, cooking utensils, food, household equipment, children, and cooks and go out camping. They travel in oxcarts and tongas. Once camp is established in a central location, the evangelists fan out

---

[16] This paragraph expresses the missiology as understood by L. S. Tracy. However, it reflects the reality of pioneering mission work, even today. Often there is confusion—sometimes chaos—a strategic plan is necessary, and the priority is "first things first", and the first priority is the message of Jesus to the world.

into the nearest villages or fairs and hold evangelistic services. They preach, teach, give tracts, and sell Bibles for a small fraction of the actual cost. Those listeners who show interest in hearing more about the gospel are invited to an inquirers' meeting held later in a central location. In these meetings, a number are genuinely converted.

As in any foreign country, the language barrier was a difficult one to overcome. Of all India's languages, Marathi (mer- AW-tee), the language of our area, is the closest to the original Sanskrit. Instead of 5 vowels, as in English, Marathi has 16. Instead of 21 consonants, it has 48. Altogether there are over 200 characters to learn. A noun has 8 cases, a verb 4 methods of agreement, and there are 17 tenses. The missionaries learned that *goose* is a rat, *mice* is a female buffalo, and *dude* is milk. Many laughable mistakes were made as the missionaries struggled to master Marathi. Lessons begun were soon discontinued when there was no money. They had to learn on their own. Money was sent to buy a pair of bullocks; a wedding present for Tracys was used to purchase an old cart. With strict frugality, it was possible to plant a little hay and grain and a few vegetables on the farm. Tracy's attempt to get the local farmers to use an iron plow for better crops was listened to politely and ignored. What had been good enough for their ancestors was certainly good enough for them. They went on using their little sticks to scratch the surface.

It is one thing to plant a field and another to find water to make it grow. The two springs on the lower end of the land dried up in the hot season. Dad hired Hindu laborers to help him dig a well 23 feet in diameter. An appeal to the American churches brought money for a pump to lift the water 40 feet to the level of the land.

Winnowing grain.
The wind blows the chaff away.

It was difficult to get men to work in the hot season, particularly on a Christian well. Time after time the sand and stone workers failed to arrive. Slowly they dug their way downward.

"Sahib (SAW-heeb)," the Hindu diggers said to Tracy one day, "the little stones fall on our bare feet and hurt us. If you will bring a coconut and sacrifice it here, nothing will happen."

"No," Dad replied, "this is a Christian field and a Christian well. God will care for us since we are His."

Within minutes, a stone dislodged from the side of the well and fell, hitting a Hindu teenage boy a sharp, glancing blow across the temple. The entire future of Nazarene missions in India hung suspended in the timeless instant that Dad leaped into the well, believing the boy was dead. The mission reputation and respect in the community was already subzero, and workmen were hard to procure. Superstition was high. And now after refusing to sacrifice a coconut to the Indian gods, and stating a faith in the Christian God, a stone had killed a boy.

But God was there. Dad carried the limp body swiftly and carefully to the town hospital, and in a week the boy was back in the muddy hole digging again.

The good, sweet water rushed in, but Dad was not satisfied. He kept digging down to 30 feet. The well averages 9 feet deep in normal times, and even in dry times it refills in the night.

The missionaries were tired. They had been in India for four years, and the last two had been a severe drain on their strength and courage. New recruits were greatly needed. The cries for help through cables and letters were answered sorrowfully, "There is no money. Hold on!" And the five held on in the dark, wide desert of idolatry and unbelievable opposition.

One scorching day in April 1908, when the temperature under the thick banyan tree in our front yard was above 107 degrees, the Tata pony mail tonga from Malkapur came to a steaming stop in front of the mission's grilled iron gates. A slender man walked unannounced up the gravel driveway and hesitated on the veranda. No one was around. It was too hot to move. Dad was trying to write foreign letters and articles in his stuffy office. The papers stuck to his wrists; the flies were unbearable. He saw a shadow on the veranda—someone for medicine, no doubt. Weary, discouraged, he wiped his face and went out.

"Brother Tracy?" asked the friendly young man.

"Yes," answered Dad with a question in his handshake.

"I am L. A. Campbell. I have come to report to you, my superintendent. With my wife and me are two others, a young man, A. D. Fritzlan, and a single lady, Miss Olive Nelson. Our churches in America are officially uniting, and we were directed to find you and associate with your mission."

He started to say more, but Dad couldn't take it. I have heard him joyfully telling the experience: "They dropped down straight from the skies," he said. "Four of them! Young! Healthy! What a colossal answer to prayer!"

Back home in America the union meeting of the Holiness Church of Christ with the Pentecostal Church of the Nazarene convened at Pilot Point, Tex., on October 8, 1908.

Dad had never been ordained. In the Journal of the General Assembly held that October day was recorded:

"Monday, October 12, Morning: The Committee on Orders ... recommended ... that Leighton S. Tracy of India ... be elected to elder's orders. The report was adopted."

He had the sanction of the church, but no elder had laid hands on Leighton S. Tracy, commissioning him to this special sacred office. The only elder among the missionaries was Rev. L. A. Campbell. It was decided that he would officiate at Dad's ordination service.[17]

The Mission Council meeting that convened in June rejoiced that the staff was back to its original number of nine

---

[17] It is quite rare for an ordination to be conducted by anyone other than a General Superintendent in the Church of the Nazarene. The ordination of Tracy was an exceptional event. Such ordinations have occurred typically in times of war, in places where security risks were high, or when too much time had passed between General Superintendent visits.

missionaries. How sorely the new members were needed became apparent within hours. Missionaries noticed that their young superintendent seemed unusually tired. He was more than tired; he was sick. It was typhoid fever. Within hours after the benediction that closed the council, Dad was in delirium. For 11 days, he lay unconscious. Messages flashed along the ocean cables, telling people at home to "Pray! Pray! Pray!"

The local government physician in Buldana, Dr. Rodgers, all but lived at the bungalow day and night. The British deputy commissioner requested hourly news and sent ice and soups, and other delicacies.

On Sunday evening, after a slight hemorrhage, he was sinking fast. We all gathered in his room to pray fervently. The doctor told us there was no hope. But God answered prayer. Dad came to and said, "I am very tired; may I rest?"

The doctor said to Julia Gibson, "Can't we all get together and pray for God to heal Mr. Tracy?"

We had been doing that, of course, but we gathered with the doctor on the veranda and asked God to heal my dad.

On Monday and on Tuesday Dad again had sinking spells, and the doctor could not help. He left the room, but he did not go home. He went into our big, old living room and fell on his knees. Brother Fritzlan found him later, on his hands and knees, wedged in between our little organ and the wall, sobbing wildly and crying to God for Dad's healing. He was never the same after that.

Dad's recovery was slow. There were two alarming relapses. Kind friends and the board sent money, and he and Mom and Grandma went up to Mount Abu, north of Bombay, where the better altitude and rest brought him back to near health again.

The effect of this miracle of healing on Buldana was electric. The people knew typhoid. As they heard of Dad's sinkings, they nodded knowingly: It was karma—fate. But then the pattern of karma was ripped in two: Tracy Sahib recovered! Prayer, said the missionaries; prayer to the one true God. Prayer, agreed the Hindus, Muslims, and Parsees; prayer to a mighty God, though they were not willing to say He was the only One. Yet He was certainly worth looking into.

This was the historical turning point of our early missionary work in India. Official opposition ceased. The bars were officially down, and the fields were open before the missionaries, white and ready to harvest.[18]

---

[18] In the early days of missions work, it is often a single event that can change the course of history. Olive Tracy believed it was the healing of her father from a serious illness that turned the tide.

First row: (left to right) Prescott Beals, Bessie Beals, John McKay,
Andrew Fritzlan, Daisy Fritzlan (holding her hat).
Back row: (left to right) Gertrude Tracy, L. S. Tracy, Eltie Muse, Amanda Mellies.

Chapter 5

In Earing Time and in Harvest Thou Shalt Rest

Exodus 34:21

It was earing time. A few shoots of green, sprouting from the long-sown seed of the gospel, began to appear.

There was Babaji Mhaske (BAW-baw-gee MHUHS-kee), of very low caste and lower reputation. He was one of the few who ventured into Julia Gibson's Sunday school in Chikhli. Lucas, the preacher working with Miss Gibson, said of those who stood outside, "They do not like our ways, Miss Sahib. They are so used to sinning and evil that it is sweet to them."

The light penetrated Babaji's mind, and he became a Christian. It was no easy thing to be the first convert, with a family and community full of relatives. Boldly he renounced his Hindu practices and asked for baptism.

The missionaries waited. They watched his changed life. Babaji learned to read. He testified to his people, and they tested him in their own way.

At last the missionaries were sure his conversion was real. The baptismal service was held at the government tank in Buldana. Rev. Campbell officiated.[19]

"Babaji," he intoned solemnly, "I baptize thee in the name of the Father, and of the Son, and of the Holy Ghost. Amen!"

L. S. Tracy baptizing a new believer

This was the great moment—the final separation between his old Hindu ways and the new Christian life. Taking a firm grasp on the big man, Brother Campbell heaved and strained to put him beneath the water. Instantly the towering Indian threw his arm around the missionary to hold him steady; surely, he must have slipped. Babaji had not been instructed in baptismal procedure. He was cautious. Chagrined, the missionary tried again, but again Babaji stood firm. "Why, the very idea!" exclaimed the distraught missionary.

---

[19] The story of Babaji illustrates a common practice in early missions. After conversion was usually a probationary period during which a convert would demonstrate genuine spiritual growth. Baptism was very big deal…a public declaration of an inner work. In India, baptism was often accompanied by the public surrendering of the symbols of the old, pre-conversion life.

On the edge of the tank smiles and snickers had developed into undisguised hilarity. Dad was nearly bursting. He handed his watch to my mother and waded into the tank. Gently he explained to Babaji the meaning of immersion in the Christian's life. "Will you let Campbell Sahib and me put you all the way under the water in token of what Christ has done for you? Are you willing?"

"Oh, yes, Sahib, oh, yes!"

And as the missionaries baptized Babaji, he nearly threw himself into the water in his eagerness.

The work grew. On January 29, 1911, the first Church of the Nazarene in India was organized at Buldana. There were two charter members and six probationers. It had to be reorganized several times, but it became a strong church.

The time came for the missionaries to take a short furlough. The Tracys and Mrs. Perry traveled overland to the tip of India, took a small ferryboat to Ceylon (now Sri Lanka), from where on March 9, 1911, they sailed to New York via Naples.

They had a few months of rest, assemblies, and deputation work. Disturbing news came from India reporting reverses; some pastors had slipped back into Hinduism. The mission board was discouraged and thought they should close the work and put their money elsewhere.[20]

"No, no, no," stormed Dad, thinking of Babaji and oth-

---

[20] One of the temptations for a denomination like the Church of the Nazarene is to "pull the plug" on difficult, failing, or stagnant missions work. However, to persevere is often—in time—the pathway to extraordinary results. India today is proof that faithfulness on the field and in the sending church can yield tremendous results in the Kingdom of God.

er tender young Christians. "There will be a harvest. Let me go back there and cultivate the seed with the others."

They sailed on October 19, 1912, with two new recruits, Miss Myrtle Mangum and Miss Lela Hargrove. They were left to work in Calcutta, while the Tracys and Mrs. Perry went on to Buldana.

All the world loves a baby. But in the Orient, given a choice, all firstborn, and perhaps second-born too, would be boys.

Dad had two daughters, and there was due rejoicing in the Christian community for each. But when Philip was born, there was great joy—a son, at last! Philip-baba, the *chota Sahib* (CHO-tuh SAW-heeb), "little master," had arrived. The temperature of respect for the mission's superintendent rose a point or two.

Baby Philip's arrival was hardly routine. In mid-November, the rains had gone, the weather was settled and pleasant, and the baby was not due for two or three weeks. Dr. Rodgers had been transferred and was not available. Mom and Dad heard of a government hospital in Jalgaon (JUHL-gown) over in the Bombay Presidency, with a good doctor.

It was getting a little late. Dad attended a holiness convention in October. Then he made a hurried trip to Calcutta, where some of the missionaries were sick.

At last Dad got back to Buldana. He then left Grandma Perry to look after the Buldana work.

Packing the family neatly into the sidecar of his motorcycle, Dad drove us to Malkapur (MUHL-kuh-poo-er), where we boarded the train to Jalgaon. There were no hotels in Jalgaon, so Mom and Dad decided to set up a camp of our own about a mile and a quarter from the hospital in a pleasant grove. In the afternoon, Dad and the cook went into town to buy groceries and camp supplies. Then they dismissed the hired cart and walked home. Everything was going beautifully; everyone was cooperating—except the baby. He decided to arrive ahead of schedule. Dad and the cook came back from the bazaar to find the camp in an uproar. Mom was in sudden pain, and Martha and I, little more than babies ourselves, were crying with misery and fear.

Leaving the cook in camp, we started down the rocky path as fast as we could go. It wasn't quite fast enough. By the time, Martha and I got to the road, Dad was frantically running ahead, calling to us to hurry, hurry.

Suddenly Dad caught up with a two-wheeled cart headed for town. Commandeering it, we tumbled in. The cart driver took one look at us and began lashing the backs of his surprised and frightened bullocks. We careened against the sides as the old cart heaved and groaned over the rocks. Dad was trying to hold Mom in his arms.

We never got to the hospital.

"I can't stand it; I can't; I can't." Mom was crying.

As we tipped around the last bend on one wheel, the Christian and Missionary Alliance bungalow came into view. Dad called to the driver to halt, leaped to the ground, threw some money to the cart driver, and raced along the rest of the road and down the long walk, carrying Mom. The Schelanders were out visiting. Bursting in, Dad found a room with a cot in it. Having been told to follow them, Martha and I pushed our way into the room. We could not understand why we were pushed back out and the door slammed in our faces. Off again Dad leaped the hedges and fence between the hospital and the mission compound. The doctor was not there. Dad made the head nurse understand his emergency. Then he was off again, back over the hedges to the mission.

He arrived at the bungalow, breathless and disheveled, just in the nick of time to bring his own son into the world. Two maiden lady missionaries hovered nervously in the background. When everything was about over, the nurse came running in and took charge. They moved Mother and her new son over to the hospital the next evening.

Standing beside Mom and the tiny little red thing they said was my brother, they tell me I studied them solemnly; then looking up at large, discolored cracks in the ceiling over the cot, I pointed and said, 'There's where he came down from heaven!"

Totally unprepared for the roars of laughter that followed, I burst into injured tears and had to be taken away. A relaxed and radiant Papa later took us back home to Buldana.

We three children gave Dad a standing invitation to all our interests and activities, but it wasn't often that he could afford time to get farther than our threshold.

"The work" was so pressing. It was paramount, demanding, absorbing. Dad would dash off on his horse, Buddy, named fondly for Bud Robinson[21], or he would pop-pop on

---

[21] Bud Robinson was an early and legendary evangelist in the Church of the Nazarene.

his motorcycle in a cloud of yellow dust, sometimes attaching the sidecar and taking us, but almost always he would go off alone to take care of "the work."

The work occupied his whole life—almost. I remember one time on vacation in the Himalayas, he took a whole day from the work, and as a family we went on a picnic to Happy Valley. We never knew we had such a playful father. He actually played games with us and laughed all day long. But it never happened again.

It was only in later years we called him Dad, because the fashion in parental titles changed to that; but when we were small, he was Papa—Papa, that tall, erect, well-built, black-haired, British Canadian gentleman who always wore glasses and a mustache. The glasses were a necessity; the mustache, a distinction. The glasses broadened a rather lean face but did not shield his eyes. They were nice eyes, friendly eyes, called gray on his passports, with an amazing trick of changing in light and shadow. They were gray-green, brown-flecked, agate eyes that reminded me of dry jungle grass at the beginning of the hot season.

> ... when we were small, he was Papa—Papa, that tall, erect, well-built, black-haired, British Canadian gentleman who always wore glasses and a mustache.

But that mustache! Always carefully clipped and trimmed, it belonged to his face. Without it he wouldn't have been Papa. In those days, no man shaved his mustache, and clean-shaven missionaries were sometimes taken for women. Very early in life we learned to watch for the slightest change of mind or mood by the tilt and expression of Papa's mustache. In disciplinary matters, it was our most reliable thermometer. Whatever the tone of his voice concealed and his eyes controlled, the mustache gave away. Stern and stiff, and we toed the mark—but let one bristle quiver ever so slightly, and it was safe to explode into whoops of hilarious laughter, in which his booming bass usually led.

Once in Calcutta we teased Dad until he finally bought us a pair of guinea pigs. We quickly accepted the responsibility of their welfare. They fascinated us for a time and flourished. Then one day we forgot to feed them. Called in from our play, we were genuinely sorry the first time and only mildly remorseful the second. But when we failed after the third warning, coax and beg and cry and plead as much as we would, we could not sway Papa one inch. We never saw the guinea pigs again or were allowed to have any more. We received, instead, a two-point lecture on cruelty to animals placed in our care, and the light breaking of promises. It stuck for life.

Martha received a pair of young bullocks as a birthday present one year. Another year, Dad gave her four peacock eggs. Under an old setting hen, two of them hatched. The beautiful birds ungratefully divided their time between the safe pigeon cote on our Christian compound and the mother-god temple half a mile away, where all day long they shared in the rich offerings made to red-painted idols, and themselves became objects of worship.

The big wooden boxes from America were perhaps our most melodramatic source of excitement. The generosity of our people was as overwhelming then as it is now, but knowledge of the appropriate and most appreciated has greatly increased with the years. The person who put those first three lollipops into the missionary box never knew that he contributed more to our Americanization than almost anyone else. We didn't know what lollipops were; they had to be explained to us. No pieces of candy ever lasted so long. We allowed ourselves one tiny lick a day, imagining that we were real American children while it lasted. And when someone packed a small piece of paraffin, Mom and Grandma didn't use it to cover jars of jelly. They showed us how Americans chewed gum. It was tasteless, but we were thrilled.

The box usually came months late for Christmas, for kind senders had no idea of the time it took en route. It arrived in the very hottest of the hot season. Our whole existence stopped. No work was done, no play pursued. Food was gulped only when we were threatened that nothing would be done until we ate. Then came the screeching of the nail puller, the *whang-whang* of the hammer, and the box stood open at last.

A quilt was on top—always! A lovely, thick, woolen patchwork, painstakingly hand-stitched, lovingly quilted, and sometimes embroidered beautifully with the names of the people of the society in the squares. Sometimes there were repaired toys; once we found a can of spoiled codfish. There was an occasional box of soggy cornflakes, some fruitcake, or packages of dried fruit, or a can of Carnation milk.

My Vermont-born mother and grandmother went into raptures over a tiny piece of maple sugar. There were often dresses of various materials and sizes packed in the middle of the box, fussily stylish, extremely old-fashioned, or just right. And very often we found quantities of underwear, long and heavy and woolly. It made our prickly heat rash itch furiously just to touch it.

We will never forget one long union suit. Dad's name was indelibly emblazoned in large letters on the front. Perhaps it was too small for him; at any rate, Dad gave it to an Indian man, a new Christian who had so little and needed so much. Thankfully, gratefully, proudly, he came to church that Sunday, wearing the Sahib's suit magnificently labeled L. S. Tracy, and topped off by his own bright red turban. I don't remember what Dad preached about that day, but all through the service his mustache twitched uncontrollably, and we children had to be forcibly ejected in disgrace.

Martha and I were more or less on our own as far as amusement was concerned. Though the Indian Christians were wonderful toward us, I'm afraid we were insufferable little monsters with them. We would dress up in their finest saris, not being too careful. We ground their peppers for curry and their grain in the stone mills very inexpertly. We slopped around to *shane* (shayn) their floors, spreading with our hands the paste-like mixture of thinned cow's dung and not doing a very good job of it. But when it was finished and dried, it was hard and glossy, clean and odorless, and about the best termite repellent there is. We lugged their babies around on our hips and hauled water from the well, balancing the big jars on our heads and spilling most of it.

We made our own dolls and cuddle toys out of old pillowcases stuffed with rags. We played jacks with pebbles, throwing one stone high and imagining it was the ball we didn't have. We climbed many trees and held long conversations with ourselves and each other in the top branches. In Buldana a thick tamarind was a playhouse, but the large banyan in front of our veranda was prime favorite.

As the first missionaries' children of our denomination, we pioneered in the matter of education. No money was sent for an allowance for schooling. Mom and Dad were determined that we should not lack formal elementary education. God provided our needs through special gifts that paid tuition and board for Martha and me at the girls' school in Calcutta for a year, then at the Presbyterian school, Woodstock, in the foothills of the Himalayas. It was high enough to provide a clean, cool, summer altitude.

For the first few years we boarded at the school built into the mountainside. Later, Mom and Grandma took turns renting cottages at Landour above Woodstock, and we slid and climbed to school each day. Many a time I was sent home with malaria, riding in a basket on the back of a coolie.

I remember clearly a lovely doll Dad and Mom brought me for a birthday present. I loved it as any little girl would, and I cried for weeks when the boarding school matron stole it and gave it to her own little girl. Dad and Mom could never afford another one for me.

Chapter 6

Behold, I Have Set the Land Before You
Deuteronomy 1:8

Dr. H. F. Reynolds made his first visit to India in April 1914. On the ship that sailed from San Francisco was a large group of missionaries under Dr. Reynolds' guardianship. Most of them were scheduled for Nazarene missionary work in China and Japan, but three young ladies were headed for India: the Misses Hulda and Leoda Grebe and Miss Virginia Roush. Miss Roush was sent to the Buldana side and did evangelistic work for four years; then her health failed, and she returned to the States.[22]

Miss Hulda and Miss Leoda Grebe, both trained nurses, were decided assets to the young mission in Calcutta.

Back in 1903 or 1904 an English lady, Mrs. Avetoom (AW-wuh-toom), started a small evangelistic work in

---

[22] Dr. H. F. Reynolds was one of the early founders of the Church of the Nazarene. He is credited with instilling in the denomination a passion for world evangelism and missions.

Calcutta.[23] Associated with her was a young Bengali widow, Mrs. Banarji (BAN-uhr-ji), who secured funds to start a small school for 16 girl widows in January 1905. The next year she contacted the Church of the Nazarene, which was led by Dr. Phineas Bresee.

Nearly a year and a half later, the New England and Pacific Coast holiness groups united in the homeland, and Leighton Tracy was sent to inspect this additional work and talk to Mrs. Avetoom and Mrs. Banarji. Sometime later, the Los Angeles church sent Mr. and Mrs. E. G. Eaton and Mr. V. J. Jacques to this area, and about this time the school was moved from the city to Hallelujah Village, a large compound in the suburbs of Calcutta.

By the time Dr. Reynolds arrived, Mrs. Avetoom had returned to England, Mr. Jacques had gone back to the States, Mrs. Banarji was leaving, and the Eatons were both very sick with malaria fever.

"They must go home at once," said Dr. Reynolds, and he sent for Dad. "Come as soon as you can pack. I'll stay with these two new nurses and the two young missionaries until you get here with your family. I'll send for a new superintendent so that you can show him around and then get back to your western India work."

For a year and a half, we lived in Calcutta. The Eatons had opened two outstations: one in Mymensingh (Ml-muhn-seengh) City, 300 miles northeast of Calcutta; and the other in the Garo (GAW-ro) Hills, another 100 miles or

---

[23] Now spelled Kolkata, reflecting its original Bengali pronunciation.

so farther north. Neither of these outstations was of much value to our work. Both areas were being adequately covered by another evangelistic denomination. Dr. Reynolds called Miss Mangum and Miss Hargrove from Mymensingh and reorganized Hope School with them in charge. Miss Hulda Grebe was put in charge of religious education, and Miss Leoda Grebe had the medical work. About a month after we moved to Calcutta, Dad went up to Mymensingh to pack up mission furnishings. From there he made the first exploratory trip to Kishorganj (KEESH-or-gunj), a city south and east of Mymensingh.

Because Dad could not speak Bengali (ben-GAW-lee), he took an interpreter along; but before they reached the nearest railway station 19 miles from Kishorganj, the interpreter came down with fever and had to return to Calcutta. For five days Dad had been eating from his lunch basket. There was only part of a tin of kippered herring and some bread left.

It was the monsoon season, and rain was coming down in torrents. A mail coach was going to Kishorganj about four the next morning. It took Dad as its only passenger, but before daylight the horses bogged down in the mud and could not go on. The mailbags and Dad were transshipped together to a boat that plied the Brahmaputra (BRA-hmuh-POO-truh) River, then transferred to another mail coach that finally reached Kishorganj.

The Kishorganj bungalow guesthouse was a poor one. Usually there are at least a caretaker and a cook of sorts, but here Dad found only a locked door. Not far away, he spotted a substantial brick building that looked as though it belonged to the government.

He went over and met the official district magistrate. Dad explained his situation, and the magistrate sent a servant to call the bungalow caretaker. Then he invited Dad to dinner. He gladly accepted.

But since he had had no breakfast, Dad asked the caretaker to find someone who would prepare a meal for him. The man came, but it was five in the afternoon before anything was ready to eat. Dad ate a little of the herring and bread in his basket and went out into the town to see if there was property for sale or rent where he could open a mission station in the center of that large area.

The next day he gathered statistics and information about the health of the district, rainfall, temperature, and so on; breakfasted with the magistrate; had tiffin[24] with the police; and then took the tonga again for the return journey about four o'clock.

Tired as he was, Dad had to walk quite a bit of the distance back to the boat because the horses could not quite make it through the mud and carry the mail too. From the boat, at three the next morning, he walked the rest of the way to Gafargaon (GUH-fuhr-gown), slept on the waiting room floor until daylight, and took the first train for Calcutta.

---

[24] "Tiffin" is a term used in India to refer to a lunch, or sometimes afternoon tea, or meal transported in a container (typically, now, made of stainless steel). The term evolved from England and is used even today in a variety of ways. In the West, one might think of a lunch box or picnic basket.

That was the very beginning of our eastern India work in Kishorganj. It was a wide-open field, but it was several years before our work there was finally established.

Rev. George Franklin was sent out to superintend the Eastern India District. He arrived August 13, 1915, and in a month, he married his friend of college days, Miss Hulda Grebe.

A month after Dad's trip to Kishorganj, he went up to inspect the work in the Garo (GAW-ro) Hills. He found the same evangelistic denomination that was in Mymensingh had extensive work here also. Dr. Reynolds and Mr. Franklin shared Dad's conclusion that we should turn our work there over to the other group and concentrate our efforts in Calcutta and Kishorganj. The Garo Hills work was closed in 1916.

I remember the mission compound in Calcutta. It had a large bungalow with an expansive flat roof. Sometimes in the hot season we used to sleep up there, under the stars. There was a wide lawn where we played badminton in the evening. Flowers, shrubs, jackfruit, and guavas grew in the garden, and tall coconut palms leaned over the irrigation tank. Bands of monkeys leaped through the trees; and all we needed to do was throw stones at them, and they would hurl coconuts at us. The boys would swim out and get the floating coconuts.

The compound had a long, grassy lane to the front gate and a light fence of some kind; but Hope School had a high, unscalable wall surrounding it, with a tiny, closely guarded postern gate that backed up against a moatlike ditch with a road beyond.

I remember one day during monsoon season, Mom took Martha and me in one of the mission gharris (GHUH-rees) (a four-wheeled cart with a top) on an errand. Dad was away on one of his many trips. As we were driving back to the mission, the front lane was flooded, and the pony could not make it through. It was getting dark. The rain was literally like curtains of water waving in the gale. Slowly the gharri splashed around to the back road and let us out at the little postern gate, then the coachman drove on to the carriage house. The usually dry ditch was flooded and running wild. The well-attended gate generally opened to us at the first call, but this night we shouted and pounded until we were hoarse. The storm snatched the cries out of our mouths. Pulling up her long, wet skirts daintily, Mom walked over to the place where we usually crossed the ditch and tested the muddy torrent. It seemed bottomless. We tried calling again, hoping someone would hear. Then abandoning all caution and propriety, Mom gathered her motherhood together and plunged in. Grabbing me, she inched her way cautiously through the black water swirling hard against us. Waist-deep, maybe almost armpit-deep, tree branches and debris striking us—and then we were across. Tossing me up the slippery bank, she went back for Martha. Then scrambling up, all three of us ran down the flooded path to the bungalow door. It flew open as we came up on the veranda, and someone with a horrified cry pulled us in to warmth and safety.

It was rare for any of us to have Dad to ourselves. One day he chose me as his sole companion on a downtown errand. Dad was driving the horse himself. I remember I chattered away about nothing for a while; then, as we passed a temple, I pointed and asked, "Papa, why don't we go in now and tear out the old idols and make the people stop worshiping them?"

This seemed to me a way far superior to holding Sunday schools, gathering orphans, and preaching in bazaars. Instantly Dad was alert.

"Do you think that would make them stop worshiping the idols?" he asked gently.

I hesitated. "Well, if they got more idols, we'd come and throw them out again."

Dad was quiet for a minute. Then he asked, "Do you think it would be better if they destroyed their own idols?"

"But they wouldn't," I said flatly. "You know they wouldn't."

This was it. This was what counted. This was why we were here. This was Christ's plan, and this was our mission, our work, our lives.

"Perhaps some of them would if we told them about Jesus and His love and they began to love Him. Then they would not want their idols and would throw them away themselves. If we went in and destroyed the idols, the people would be angry at us and would worship the idols all the more. But if they learned to love Jesus, they wouldn't want the idols anymore. That would save us the trouble of always having to come down here and throw the idols out. Wouldn't that be better?"

"Ye-e-s," I admitted reluctantly.

It was less colorful and exciting than my way, but I could see that his idea was better. And for the first time, I saw the point of having Sunday schools and orphanages, and preaching, and giving medicine, and visiting, and raising the economic standard of living. This was it. This was what counted. This was why we were here. This was Christ's plan, and this was our mission, our work, our lives.

Chapter 7

Ye Shall Sow the Land

Genesis 47:23

In western India, the plan of touring took hold. We got back to Buldana from Calcutta at the start of the touring season, and the whole family went touring, babies and all. Babies were an asset, making no difference in the schedule. "A man with a family is more respected than one traveling alone," Dad said.

We made quite an encampment when we all went together, for it was essential that the Indian preachers bring their wives and families along too, and we attracted about as much attention as a traveling carnival. Everything was a curiosity: our clothing, cooking utensils, camp cots, and the little folding canvas chairs. Dad's typewriter was a thing of great wonder in their sight. On tour, he would write his articles and letters with circles of admiring men and boys watching every finger motion, delighted with the tinkle of the little bell at the end of each line.

In addition to the humans and their camp equipment, there were all the animals, carts, and fodder. Four camps were usually established in one season, centralizing the work in the most interested areas and branching out from there into surrounding villages.

Touring was a highlight in our lives. Living in the tent, often pitched under thick trees with bands of rhesus or han uman (HAWN-oo-mun) monkeys racing and swinging over us or screaming and fighting for choice perches before settling down to a chattery night, was uproarious fun for us. Why the grownups threw sticks and pebbles at the thieving marauders we never understood.

When the great mud-colored beasts bounded away at last, it was only natural that we tied ropes to our waists for tails and went leaping through the same branches in ungraceful imitation. Poor little Phil was too small to climb, and he used to stand on the ground so wistful and unhappy, with his little rope tail dragging pitifully in the dust.

Occasionally we camped near water where we could splash and paddle with as much abandon as our big, ever-present pith helmets allowed us. Once on tour at Hatedi (HAW-terd-ee), my mother was roused in the night with an unexplainable premonition. The next morning, we all went out to see a cow that had been killed by a panther about three-quarters of a mile from our tent.

There was always preaching in the villages. In the cool of the day we would go to a central place; Mom pumped the little organ, and everyone sang. Dad and the Indian preachers would talk and show pictures on big cards and give out tracts and sell Scripture portions. In later years Dad had a magic lantern.[25] The night would blossom in brightness and color as familiar stories appeared on a spread sheet, and Dad's deep voice in flowing Marathi told the story of Jesus and His love.

There was not always easy acceptance of the gospel. In the Mogalai (MO-guh-law-ee) area, about 30 miles from Buldana, was the town of Anwa (AWN-waw). In 1913, some of the Indian preachers went touring into this territory on an evangelistic trip. Six days they stayed in Anwa, welcomed with open arms and entertained in the homes with the best hospitality the villagers could provide. So eager were the people of this village for the gospel that men would not go to their day's work and collect their wages, preferring to stay and listen. When the Indian preachers finally left, most of the people followed half a mile or more beyond the village limits, wept at parting, and begged them to return.

The touring party came back to Buldana with glowing reports of this village. It did not work out for a missionary to visit Anwa immediately. Dad had to go to Calcutta and was away for a year and a half. When he returned, he felt he had to get close to the people. He thought that if he could live with them, eat what they eat, and talk to them in their homes, he could reach more people.

Dad had an Indian turban wound on his pith sun helmet and put on other Indian garments; then, with some gospel portions and tracts, a black umbrella, a roll of blankets, a

---

[25] A "magic lantern" was an early version of a projector to show slides. The light was generated by kerosene fuel and a mirror. No electricity was available.

brass plate, and a *lota* (LOW-tuh)[26] drinking vessel, he set off on a three-week tour accompanied by two Indian preachers.

They went from village to village on foot, sitting on the ground around the dried-dung fires at night, looking deep into men's hearts. They came at last to Anwa.

"These are the people who welcomed the Christians before," Dad remembered; "perhaps they are ready for baptism by now."

News travels fast in India, and the movements of the three men had been leisurely and open. Even as they passed under the thick arched gateway, they sensed hostility. With sullenness and almost open enmity, the villagers reported that all for whom the Sahib inquired were away.

"No, that one is not here. ... He also has gone from the village. ... No, Sahib, I do not know where. ... When will he return? Who knows! ... No, there is no place for you to stay. ... Yes, there is a bed, that one. ... Food? You may buy these cold *chapattis* (chuh-PAWT-tees)[27] and a little *lonsi* (LONE-see)."

Out under a tamarind tree between the village and the river, Dad set up camp between two carts. It was Saturday night and cold for India. A sharp wind, though broken by hung blankets, made his bath an unpleasant ordeal. The bed, a wooden frame strung with ropes and no mattress, was far too short and alive with vermin. The oily, pepper-hot, green-mango *lonsi*, wrapped in a cold, unleavened *chapatti* flat cake, was like lead in his stomach.

---

[26] Lota is a small vessel, typically for water, made of brass or copper.

[27] Chapattis are simple Indian flatbread, common everywhere on the sub-Continent.

A beautiful Sunday morning dawned. The air was cool and crisp. It reminded him of a late summer day in his Canadian boyhood, and he could almost imagine himself going off to the little holiness Sunday school in Hartland, dressed in his best suit. And just over the hill was the church.

But there was no hill, no church—just a cold, gray wall and a shut gate. Anwa, that had been so warm! Anwa, that was so cold they had cast him out! Anwa, that would not even give him the traveler's courtesy of sleeping in their inn!

He sat on the bed with a great burden for the town and area, crying like a baby, with disappointment and homesickness and joy all mixed together. Joy that he knew he was in the center of God's will in the heart of India, homesickness to hear one word in his own language, and disappointment that the villagers would not receive him. For a long time, he sat praying for the people who had turned him out. And at last, the call emerged, standing alone against the gray walls and closed gate of Anwa.

> Joy that he knew he was in the center of God's will in the heart of India, homesickness to hear one word in his own language, and disappointment that the villagers would not receive him.

In Dad's pocket was a little harmonica that he had bought in some bazaar. He reached for it. The Holy Spirit was so comfortingly near, the call so clear. Suddenly he stumbled on the refrain of the old, old song,

And when the battle's over,
We shall wear a crown
In the new Jerusalem.

At that instant, the tumult in his heart died, and the glory of the Lord filled the temple of his soul. It rolled over and over him in waves of emotion. The victory *would* come to Anwa; in fact, it was by faith already here. Again and again, he played the beautiful melody, tears of joy coursing his tired face. That village gate *was* open to the gospel—he knew it!

The weeks and months and years went by. A toehold was gained at last. A tiny church. Another. Another. After Dad returned home to retire, the whole Mogalai began to open up.

Jamner (ZHAWM-neer) was opened late in 1912. Another mission had been operating in that section, but by 1910 they asked us to take it over if we wished. Miss Hitchens and Miss Nelson, at Igatpuri (EE-guht-poo-ree), were interested and wanted to go touring at once in the area.

"All right," Dad said, "I'll meet you there with the camping equipment."

For propriety's sake, Mom went along and took the baby. They loaded the creaky old mission cart with mountains of baggage and started out the morning of December 7, 1910, planning to hire bullocks at every village and send the tired animals back to their owners. It was a 43-mile trip. All went well for about 2 miles. Not yet down to the plain, one of the crude iron tires of the cart worked loose from the wheel and wobbled crookedly off the road and into the ditch. Long experience with this common malady of carts had taught

Dad what to carry at all times. Out came the ax, and they pounded the tire on again. At the first stream, the wooden wheel swelled enough to take care of it nicely. But somehow the indispensable ax was left on the road or slipped out, and everything had to stop while someone went back to find it.

At the first village, fresh bullocks were hired, but scarcely a mile beyond, one of the animals lay down in the road and refused to go on. Dad sent back to the village for another. Before they reached the third village, this had happened three times with three different bullocks. By dusk they reached the third village, where the people generously supplied them with *chapattis* and a *lota* of rich milk. As they slept in the three-sided open inn, a bullock lumbered into the shelter, upsetting things in its path. Dad got up and drove it out. When they started the next morning, the body of the old cart began to slide along the axle against one wheel. As they went down a steep bank into a river, one side of the yoke stuck down into the mud and broke off, and the bullock scrambled free. Then came three miles of riding up over boulders and down into ruts. The girder above the axle split from the strain. Fortunately, they were near a village, and a carpenter fixed it with a pole lashed on like a splint. By afternoon of the third day they crawled into Jamner.

I asked my mother how they made the return trip.

"We spent Christmas up there," she remembered. "I went into Bhusawal (bhoo-SAW-wuhl) on the train and bought a few gifts. They must have fixed the cart somehow. I don't remember the trip back. Your father was pretty handy at fixing things, you know."

By 1912 Miss Olive Nelson was sent to Jamner. With her went a friend, Miss Pearl Simmons, an independent associate. Miss Nelson and Miss Simmons rented a house in the town and began evangelistic work. Hardly had they arrived and settled in their new home when Miss Simmons took sick very suddenly. As Dad and Mom and Grandma landed in Calcutta on their way back from their first furlough, a telegram was handed them at the pier. "Simmons very sick—smallpox." She had contracted the disease from a bullock cart driver they had hired. Confluent hemorrhagic smallpox is a highly contagious and dreaded disease. Great running, bleeding sores eat at the skin and the vital parts of the body.

As soon as the news reached Buldana, Brother Fritzlan and a new missionary, Miss Daisy Skinner, went up to help. The three missionaries did their best to help the sick woman, but a few days after the rash appeared, the disease took her life. Brother Fritzlan secured a bit of land from the headman of the town, and in the center of the plot they dug the grave. In India, with a disease of this nature, burial has to be as swift as possible to prevent any spreading to epidemic proportions. Miss Simmons passed away about midnight, December 13, 1912. The missionaries held a short service, and before dawn she had to be laid away. Some months later a flat, full-length stone, carved from white marble, was finished and laid on her grave.

Since no missionary could be sent to Jamner to stay permanently, the grave became neglected, and dust blew over it and obliterated all signs of its existence. Twenty years later, word came from the Indian preacher in Jamner that a shrine was slowly growing at the missionary's grave. Wind and monsoon rain had uncovered one of the corner markers, and Muslim women passing along a footpath near noticed it. Scraping around with a stick, they laid bare part of the gravestone with strange, carved messages in a language unknown to them. They were sure that a *peer*[28] was coming up from the earth. They began worshiping there and leaving small offerings to appease the spirit and persuade it to go away. Someone from Buldana went up to Jamner, cleaned off the rest of the stone, and explained to the people what it was, and the shrine was cleared away.[29]

In the summer of 1913, Rev. A. D. Fritzlan and Miss Daisy Skinner were married. They went up to Jamner to continue the work, but they had to return to Buldana when Dad had to go to Calcutta.

Jamner marked the northwestern extremity of our district, and Mehkar (MAY-huh-kur) was in the southeastern corner. In 1912, the Campbells went down to Mehkar.

They rented a squalid little house, scarcely more than a hut. A little girl was born there, and with their three boys made quite a houseful. They had much sickness in Mehkar. Their second son, a boy of four, died in 1914. There is a

---

[28] A *peer* in this context is an object that rises from the earth as an erect stone or stump, which was believed to be a place of divine presence and encounter.

[29] The story of Miss Pearl Simmons can be used to illustrate the life and death of hundreds of pioneering missionaries. It is on their work and sacrifice that today's harvest is built. They lie buried in the soil of the lands to which God called them, but from their faithfulness springs many fruits.

price to the consecration of a missionary. The Campbells returned to America in 1915, and an Indian preacher was stationed in Mehkar.

Shortly after Jamner and Mehkar were first opened, World War I was raging in Europe. Prices began to soar. Important correspondence went down in torpedoed ships and had to be re-sent in duplicate and triplicate. Cables were tied up or destroyed. Suspicion shadowed everyone. Dad, a British-Canadian subject, was called to the service. With our hearts sinking, Dad went up to Akola (uh-KO-luh) to report. There the medical examination found that he had varicose veins and would be unfit for the infantry, but there were other duties he could be made to perform. For weeks, we did not know what the outcome would be. Then there came an order from government that all British missionaries were to be exempt from active duty. Each was requested to return to his station and hold the country in check as effectively as possible. They could best serve their nation by discouraging any local trouble, thus relieving the empire of the necessity of retaining troops there. So, like a clump of grass planted at the top of a possible landslide, Dad went back to his station, put his roots of influence down deep, and held on.

When Dr. Reynolds made his first world tour of Nazarene missions in 1914,[30] one of his important stops was at Khardi (KHUHR-dee) in the Thana (THAW-nuh)

---

[30] After Dr. Reynolds' first world tour of Nazarene missions in 1914, a union of several US holiness groups occurred. In India, this meant the creation of a single, stronger district in Maharashtra. Rev. Roy Codding was named the first superintendent there. His great desire was that it be a "fusion" rather than just a union.

District of the Bombay Presidency, 60 miles northeast of Bombay. Earlier on his trip, Dr. Reynolds had developed a policy for the work in Japan. Now he led the missionaries in India in developing a similar policy for the work in that country. The mission policies for Japan and India became a template for a general missions policy adopted by the General Board of Foreign Missions to cover all fields. Meanwhile, the Pentecostal Mission of Nashville, under Rev. J. O. McClurkan, had established a thriving work there in 1903. In Khardi were Rev. and Mrs. Roy Codding; in Vasind, Miss Eva Carpenter; and in Murbad, Miss Jessie Basford. Dr. Reynolds returned to the States to use his influence to unite this fine body of people with the Church of the Nazarene. The next year, the Stateside bodies united, and the two districts in India became one in June 1915. At the special assembly on July 21, Rev. Roy Codding was chosen as superintendent; he said his great desire was that it be a "fusion" rather than just a union. Representatives from the three sections of this new district were present; Buldana, where they met; Calcutta; and Khardi.

One of the first acts after the union was to bring the boys from the Dhamandari property in Buldana to Khardi. Brother Codding became seriously ill and had to return to America late in 1917.

It seems as though most missionaries have spent their lives moving. We were no exception. When Coddings left, the Tracys moved to Khardi, which was a pleasant place. It was on the railroad and close to Bombay and Igatpuri. There was a fine, cactus-enclosed compound; a long, sloping walk up to the main bungalow; another bungalow nearby; and plenty of room for the school and other buildings. The enclosure was planted with shade trees and fruit trees: limes, lemons, mangoes, bananas, and papaya. Lovely Rangoon creeper vines grew profusely over the veranda, swinging their full clusters of pendant pink and white blooms. From our small hilltop, we could see the Western Ghats almost circling the horizon.

We had been living in Khardi for six or eight months when the mission board at home decided to close the boys' school. It came as a shock to Dad; for, though the school was not showing the gains it should, Dad was getting things in better functioning order. Most of the boys were moved back to Buldana, and Dad was left free to do full-time evangelism.

No day in a missionary's life is typical. Each one comes fully furnished with its own new, unusual, and completely unexpected events. Just such a day was one Sunday in Khardi. It began with a visit to a man in the village suffering from a septic sore. Dad had to stay and drink tea with the hospitable and grateful relatives.

A stop at a Sunday school meeting in a village cowshed warmed his heart as he listened to a class of boys learning the Lord's Prayer and other verses. In the men's class, he heard the local pastor forcefully expounding James 1:22. Grabbing a man squatting on the ground nearest him, the preacher peered into his ear to see if there was a hole straight through. "If anyone hears with one ear and lets it out with the other," the preacher said, "he must be empty-headed, and it will be seen.

"God has given us this fanlike thing outside of our heads," he went on, pulling the fellow's ear, "and He has given us an apparatus inside our heads to transmit the sound to our brains," hitting the fellow's head a sharp swat. "And we are expected to remember and practice the Word that we hear."

Chuckling at the demonstration, Dad went back to the bungalow to prepare for the afternoon meeting. After the service a woman asked to have two troublesome teeth pulled. So, Dad put down his Bible, got out the forceps, asked the woman to sit down on the ground, and had the teeth out in short order.

In the evening service held in the cow shed, the crowd was a bit slim. Then Dad found out that a troupe of popular ballad singers was in town. He invited them in to the service and asked them to sing for the combined audience, specifying that it be a clean song, not one of the lurid type common to such itinerants. To his surprise they sang a hymn, "What Does Salvation Mean?" Delighted, Dad borrowed their folding organ and sent for Mom. As she played, they enjoyed a singspiration of Christian songs. Then he preached to the motley congregation.

A satisfying compensation comes to a missionary when he can win someone "at Samaria's well," preach to a congregation of one and tell the wonderful story of Jesus, the story of love. Love! It was an innovative thought to the Hindu mind. Who ever heard of a God who did not get angry for some abstract, preposterous reason, who always listened to prayers without having to be awakened with dinging bells to accept a handful of grain or some other small offering to tangibly convey the idea to the idol that a petition was being asked!

"Love is the more excellent way," said Indian District Superintendent S. J. Bhujbal, speaking to the missionaries at their Council Meeting. "The Indian church loves you. I request you missionaries to love them in return. Love is the link between God and the sinner. When His love is shed abroad in our hearts, we cannot help but love. Revival will come through this more excellent way. Victory will be won through this great love."

Love was Dad's whole life, his only message to the Indian people. I recall sitting near an open window that looked out on our veranda in Khardi and listening to Dad talk to an old, old man who had tottered painfully into the compound for a little medicine. Someone had told him that the missionary would help him. When Dad had done what

> Love was Dad's whole life, his only message to the Indian people.

he could for the man's deep sores, he sat down cross-legged on the matting in front of the man and began telling him slowly and simply about Jesus and His love. "What do you say?" the man asked. "I do not understand. Yesu (YAY-shoo) Crist (CREEST)? What do you say Yesu Crist will do for me?"

Patiently Dad went over it again.

"Why have I never heard of this new God before?" he quavered. "I am an old man; I cannot understand. Why did not someone tell me sooner?"

"I could not come before," Dad replied sadly; "but whenever you are in trouble or dying, call on Yesu Crist. Remember the name, Yesu Crist."

"Yesu Crist?" He trembled as he got to his feet, and stood a minute swaying before starting down the path.

"Yes. When in trouble, call on Yesu Crist. Yesu Crist."

Halfway to the gate, he turned and looked back.

Yesu Mata? (YAY-shoo MAW-taw) he called painfully, and I recognized the name of the smallpox goddess of the Gonds, a Dravidian people of central India.

"No, no, old man! Yesu *Crist*, Yesu *Crist*, Yesu *Crist*!"

And he went slowly out of the gate and down the road, muttering, "Yesu Crist, Yesu Crist."

Dad stood a long time on the veranda, and then to himself he said softly, "'Whosoever shall call upon the name of the Lord shall be saved.' Perhaps I'll meet you over there after all, old man. Then you will understand."

When Dad came into the bungalow, there were tears running down his cheeks.

Chapter 8

His Word Was in Mine Heart as a Burning Fire
Jeremiah 20:9

Grandma was a giant; Grandma was a tiny little moth of a thing. Grandma was a tower of iron; Grandma was soft and gentle and consumed with compassion for the sick and those in trouble. Rigid in discipline, austere, keen, quick, wiry, alert to wrong, stern, and solid as the rock-bound coast of her New England, Grandma lived strictly by rule and principle.

She sometimes had to take full charge of us when we were young, and then we often felt her unpliant corrections impressed smartly on us. Sputter as defiantly as we would, our quick flares of temper went out abruptly like half-burned matches before the hurricane of her chastisements. Grandma sewed for us. She bound up our little hurts. She told us long stories of her Vermont childhood: about cold, swift mountain streams and the woolen mills where her father was chemical dyer, and tales of her country schoolhouse. There wasn't much we could understand. But we knew the look in her bright blue eyes; and, if we pressed hard enough, she would tell the stories all over again, to our delight. Most of the time we ran around barefoot, but on Sundays it was our cross to have to wear shoes and heavy-ribbed stockings. Grandma, realizing our irritability and pinched and itching feet, would read to us, entertaining away the long afternoons until bedtime and Monday morning came to our release.

Grandma was a tower of iron; Grandma was soft and gentle and consumed with compassion for the sick and those in trouble.

Grandma Ella Winslow Perry was born in Weathersfield, Vt., on June 20, 1856. She was not quite 19 years old when she married Nathan Perry, a young minister. And she became a widow at 28 with two small children when her young husband died of pneumonia. Sometime between his death and his funeral, Grandma flung herself unreservedly into the arms of God and was sanctified. She never wavered from that time on. Her faith held her steady as she took in sewing for 17 years to educate her boy and girl. It supported her when her son was drowned when he was a young and gifted teacher. This same consecration compelled her to India.

A clear, hot fire of love for the sick of India transformed itself into the energy and high candlepower of her life expended for them. With no formal training as a nurse, she would listen intently, getting the gist of their Marathi as they talked, examine their sick bodies, then go into her dark little dispensary hut, read the books, and mix her own remedies. With the combination of her drugs and her prayers, most of her patients recovered. According to the records Grandma compiled annually for the government, we estimate that during her years as a missionary Grandma ministered to nearly 10,000 different individuals.

I have quite an album of mental pictures of Grandma. Some were given me by Dad and Mom, and some vividly remembered: Grandma going to her dark closet to pick up a blouse that had dropped to the floor and putting her hand on the coils of a sleeping cobra; Grandma trying to cross a shallow river on stepping-stones, losing her balance and falling in, to her chagrin and our huge delight; Grandma stuffing cushions with the silky fuzz of the kapok tree; Grandma cooking, sewing, making jelly from roselle calyxes; Grandma, staunch American, getting out her big old recipe book with a picture of Old Glory on its cover and propping it up over the door because it was the Fourth of July, and we had no other flag with which to celebrate.

Grandma generally went touring with us, taking her medicines with her and giving out her remedies and ointments and poultices wherever she went. Dad often laughingly said that she caught more people for potential Christians with her quinine pills and castor oil than he did with preaching and distributing tracts.

We lived in Khardi in the Thana District near Bombay during the last days of Grandma's life—the only white people in town. Grandma, just past 62 then, seemed to be ripening for heaven. The terrible heat bothered her a great deal; then came the rains, the cool season, and Christmas. It was around that time that Phil and I came down with chicken pox. Phil had recovered and I was getting better when Dad and Mom decided to go to Bombay on business, taking Martha and Phil with them. The bungalow was quiet and lonely after they had gone, and I began to cry. Grandma took my temperature, asked me how I felt, and then said, "Would you like to catch up with them and go to Bombay too? I think we can make it if we hurry."

We hurried, and the surprise we gave the others waiting on the platform just as the train pulled in was half the trip to me. We shopped, ate at a nice restaurant, and went home tired but very happy.

That was the trip where Grandma contracted the Asiatic cholera, which had reached mild epidemic proportions in the city. We did not know it, of course, at the time. But a little while later she did not feel well; and while she was lying down, a man came from the village, asking for medicine.

There was gratitude mixed with scalding tears ...

Grandma got up and went to the door to give it to him; but as she handed him the salve, she fell at his feet in a dead faint. Martha and I saw her fall and ran screaming into the house. Dad and Mom came quickly, lifted her, and laid her gently on her bed.

Symptoms of cholera developed rapidly. Mom and Dad did the best they could, following directions in the medical books and easing her suffering as much as possible. When she knew she was going, she asked to be buried on the hillside behind the bungalow, "as the Indians are buried." That meant wrapping the body in a sheet and lowering it into a crude, unlined grave.

"No," said Dad, "we'll take you to Igatpuri." She seemed satisfied. She spoke a great deal about Jesus, her Friend, anticipating the joy of seeing Him. At eight o'clock that evening, just 28 hours after she fell at the feet of the Indian man, Grandma went to meet her Friend.

There was gratitude mixed with scalding tears as Mom and Dad washed and dressed the frail little body: joy and gratitude that she had made the landing on the other side, tears that she could not stay with us any longer. Tenderly they placed her on the only conveyor available, an old door, wrapped now in sheets. We children had used it to slide down the grassy hill in play. It was our door, and we were heartbrokenly glad to have something to give for Grandma's use. Mom and Dad washed and disinfected everything in the room, taking her bedding, mattress, and clothing out to a pit and burning and burying them all.

"Blessed are the dead which die in the Lord" (Rev. 14:13), Grandma had read from her Scripture portion from the promise box at our last family prayer. "Blessed are the dead which die in the Lord," repeated Dad chokingly, with tears streaming down his seamed face. Then with words of hope and joy he told us briefly of the glorious fulfillment of a life consecrated wholly to the service of her Master. He prayed—a broken, almost wordless prayer—and it flowed around us, a sweet, healing balm, a fragrance reaching deep into our sore and empty hearts.

When our service was over, Dad and one of the young preachers took her body in the tonga on the long, 21-mile trip to Igatpuri, while Mom and we three children went up on the train. We had another service at a missionary home there, and then a number of kind Christian friends followed the little hand-drawn cart up the hill to the Church of England cemetery for the committal service.

There is a tree that grows beside Grandma's grave. It is called the jasmine tree, the temple tree. But I like the name the people of Ceylon (now Sri Lanka) have given it: the life tree, for it will burst into leaf and flower even if it is pulled up from the soil—an emblem of immortality. Only a few weeks during the hot season it does not bloom. All the rest of the year it blossoms continuously, spreading its long, narrow leaves and dropping its waxy-white, yellow-throated flowers like curled, five-petaled magnolias on her grave. And there they lie, a blanket of beauty, fresh, fragrant, holding life and perfume longer than any other flower known—until that day when Grandma no longer will need the grave but will answer the clarion trumpet call to meet her Lord in the skies.

There are times in the lives of all servants of God when the zeal for Christian service, the passion for souls, and the call become a white-hot composite of burning intensity. But the body cannot keep pace; it must retire for a while—it must take a furlough. To some this period is a torture; they must get back to their field at once. They cannot adjust to their homeland. Away too long, their place at home is filled; they are strangers.

To others a furlough is a thrilling adventure. Dad plunged headfirst into his second furlough. True, there was a sharp feeling of aloneness—no one met us at the pier. But the bay fog lifted suddenly, and the bells of a hundred churches chimed the ship through the narrowing water, calling a Sunday welcome. We had landed in San Francisco.

It was a strange world to all of us. "Garages!" Dad exclaimed as he noted numbers of them from the train windows. "What in the world is a garage?"

Gradual growth can seem sharply abrupt when one is catapulted into a world advanced suddenly into the future.

To us children everything was bizarre, as though we wore trick glasses. Money—I was afraid of it. What were dollars and pennies and quarters and nickels and dimes! People on the street stopped to look at us, our strange clothes, perhaps, or maybe our India-yellow coloring from so much malaria and quinine. They laughed out loud at our strange accents. In school our classmates hooted at us, needling us into a stream of Marathi protest that amused them hugely. We felt like insects impaled on the point of a pin, struggling.

Most of the deputation Dad did alone or with another missionary. We were glad. We did not like sitting on the platform or the front seats, dressed in costumes, and feeling like prize calves at a county fair on display.

For about eight months Dad toured the country, speaking on India. Then he took the pastorate offered him in Burns, Oregon. "I felt I wanted to get my family into a colder climate to thicken their blood," our Canadian father wrote to a friend. In that desire, he certainly succeeded. For those two winters the thermometer stayed near 20 below with a few dips to 40, and there was generally two or three feet of snow on the ground.

It was a wonderful, adapting, adjusting, Americanizing two years. But education was Dad's consuming passion. He had missed so much formal schooling in his youth, and he wanted to learn so much. In India, he bought books about the country, the crops, missionary advancement, oriental philosophy, religions, music, and other areas. In America, he wrote Dr. H. Orton Wiley, president of Northwest Nazarene College in Nampa, Idaho; but there was no employment there then, no means of supporting his family.

While pastoring in Burns, Dad wrote for a correspondence course. It was fine but not enough. Then the college called him; they needed a principal for the academy. So, we moved to Nampa in an old 1919 Dodge car, and Dad taught general science besides being principal, and Mom taught two academy English classes.

Dad built a house for us near the college that first summer. When the garage was finished, we moved in. Then when the basement was completed, we moved there. At last the house was far enough along for a final move. I remember endless canning for the winter's food. Anything that was cheap we put up in jars.

We all went to school. The main object of our Nampa sojourn was Dad's education. Never having gone to high school, he had no diploma. His credits earned at Pentecostal Collegiate Institute were inadequate. The college authorities called him in. Language? Not Latin or Greek, but he had studied Sanskrit from an Indian pundit[31]; not French or Spanish, but Marathi rolled easily from his tongue, and he had a working knowledge of Bengali and could understand a little Hindustani. Good! They went down the list of requirements, gave an examination or two, and gave him credit for two years of college. Mom had high school plus a freshman year at the University of Vermont. So, they credited her with another year of college, and they both enrolled as juniors.

Salaries started and stopped with the school year. In the summer, we were on our own. We made up a crew and went to the fruit belt. There were cherry orchards in Idaho; then up to Washington for peaches, pears, plum, apples; and once, when there was nothing else, we picked hops. Setting up our tents in the orchards, we all worked. We did anything for a little money to go to school!

For Dad, the payoff came in the classroom. Sitting at the feet of the great theologian H. Orton Wiley was the culmination of years of scholastic yearning. He took every course under President Wiley that he could.

In June 1924, three diplomas were handed to the Tracys. It was a gala day when Dad and Mom received their bachelor of arts degrees with the caps and gowns and hoods. On the same day my sister, Martha, graduated from the academy. We stayed in Nampa a year longer; then the lure of more education moved us east. Traveling in the old Dodge,

---

[31] This term was used for a person who is considered an expert in a particular subject, and often was a 'tutor' in the language. It comes from the Hindi word 'pandit', the Sanskrit 'pandita', which means scholar.

we camped in tents the whole summer across the States as Dad scheduled missionary meetings. We ended our long trek in front of the portico of Eastern Nazarene College in Wollaston, Mass. Here we bowed our heads, and Dad thanked God for the safe trip, then commended his daughters to further divine care. We climbed out of the car, and there in the gravel driveway we divided our goods; for Martha and I were to enroll here, and Dad and Mom and Phil were to go on. After this, except for occasional summer vacations, we never lived together as a united family.

The Kennedy School of Missions[32] is a large branch of the Hartford Seminary Foundation, and down into Connecticut Mom and Dad and Phil went. Dad and Mom earned their master of arts degrees, majoring in missions, and felt prepared at last to give their best to the Master's service in India. But there was a delay. For three years Dad pastored the Binghamton, N.Y., Church of the Nazarene while he waited.

On December 7, 1929, they sailed on the Anchor Line. The same church that had farewelled and welcomed them many years ago was again saying farewell. I felt it couldn't possibly be happening again to us.

The people were fluttering around us, promising prayers, promising help, promising to invite us to see them. But the well of my self-pity went deep. This was

---

[32] The Kennedy School of Missions was for many decades a premier center for mission training and thought. Dr. Paul Orjala, pioneer missionary to Haiti, and founder of the missions program at Nazarene Theological Seminary, in Kansas City, earned his PhD from this school and seminary.

not *my* call, *my* consecration, *my* sacrifice—or was it? Then they melted away to leave us alone as a family.

We went down to the cabin. Dad prayed quietly, scarcely more than a broken whisper, commending us again into God's keeping. He and Mom held us each close in their arms one last instant—then the loud gongs clanged through the passageways, pushing us along in front of their din until they swept us, like so much unwanted refuse, out on the pier.

We stood there, dazed, vaguely aware that the ship was pulling away, and we waved mechanically until there was just a blur of faces along the rail. For a few minutes we missed Phil, then found him on the other side of the pier, gazing vacantly at nothing—Phil, just in his teens, needing his father so much.

The papers were filled with news of heavy storms in the North Atlantic, but our first word from Mom and Dad was a cable: They had had a smooth crossing and expected to spend Christmas in London.

Time is credited with taking care of everything, and in a way, it does. We changed the pattern of our lives. We found things to occupy us. We graduated with just ourselves as family to clap when we got our diplomas. We located small jobs in the jobless depression years. And time brought, eventually, the perception that it *was* our call, and certainly our consecration and sacrifice. We had helped Dad and Mom in the past, and we weren't going to let them down now. The work always came first in India, and it still must have top priority.

With the resilience of youth, we dried the tears in our hearts, wrote long, newsy, cheerful letters, sent packages and snapshots, and did our best to look forward to the grand time when the folks would be home, home, home with us again.

During their long stay in the States, changes had taken place in India. Seventeen new missionaries had been sent in a span of two years. Some stayed for short terms and returned home. Miss Viola Willison died. Dr. H. F. Reynolds visited India again in 1921, and Dr. George Sharpe of Scotland, appointed missionary superintendent, visited India twice before dwindling funds caused the office to be discontinued. The Coddings, Franklins, and Fritzlans returned from furloughs. In a short time, Brother Codding's health failed, and they had to return to the States. Eva Carpenter and Jessie Basford left in 1920.

There was constant moving of missionaries to staff the vacated mission stations.

In a tragic auto accident on November 22, 1928, Mrs. Fritzlan was seriously injured, and their baby, Horace, was killed. They spent a year in London recovering, but Mrs. Fritzlan never regained the complete healing of her right arm. They had given a total of 21 years of service to India when they finally returned home.

In 1919 Brother Fritzlan and Dad conducted a few meetings near the Mogalai (MO-guh-law-ee) border in which several members of a caste of robbers had been saved. Robbery to them was a hereditary and honorable profession. It was their sole business. While Dad was home on furlough, Brother Fritzlan continued to work with them.

One day he looked out of the window of his home in Buldana to see several handcuffed prisoners being taken to the jailhouse down the road. He was much surprised to see some of his new converts in the group. He went over to investigate. He was told that a robbery had been committed in the area of their village, and they had been arrested on general principles based on their past records.

"Sahib," the police said, "we are tired of these men. We can do nothing with them. For years, they have been a constant trouble to us. They fill up our jails. They are no good. Now they say they have become Christians and are no longer thieves. Sahib, if this is true, we give them to you. If they plunder and rob, you will be responsible. They are yours."

So great was the faith of the missionary in the work of grace wrought in the hearts of these men that he not only took the risk and responsibility for their behavior but also gave them housing in his backyard and taught them honest trades. Twice each night the police came along the road behind their quarters, calling the roll and waking the men to answer. They continued to do this for more than a year before the police were convinced that the men were genuine Christians. For more than 30 years (at last count) these men have remained true to God. Not one has gone back to his old trade.

As Dad and Mom traveled by train and ship back to India, Dad thought ahead to the work awaiting him. His scribbled notes reveal the pattern of his thoughts:

Encourage a spirit of prayer.

Encourage a feeling of responsibility in pastors and churches.

Encourage spiritual singing, using Indian music.

Develop camp meetings and conventions.
Develop translation and publication of holiness literature.
Hospital and school buildings.
Find how to accomplish more with less money.
Study the life of the people.
Do not fossilize.

Dad felt keenly that it was time to advance and build, to journey on to the full establishment of the church.

Chapter 9

Mine Eyes Shall Be upon the Faithful of the Land

Psalm 101:6

On October 29, 1929, Wall Street crashed, and depression covered the world like a swift, paralyzing ice storm. Overnight, money was frozen, fortunes disappeared, and banks closed their doors never to open again. Securities vanished, organizations were ruined, and millions of people were in poverty and utterly destitute. Most churches suffered acutely though managing to survive, but many of their branch mission stations died.

Dad and Mom, already under appointment, left on schedule just 39 days after the big crash. The crippling effects of the recession, the withdrawals and recalls began almost as soon as they arrived in India. The council met in January and elected Dad superintendent over his protests. General Superintendents Goodwin and Williams presided. News from home was definitely alarming. Mission money was dwindling; the people didn't have it to give. It seemed impossible to maintain what the mission fields already had. Consolidation was happening everywhere.

The council deliberated. Thana District would have to close at once. McKays must come from Khardi and Miss Mellies and Miss Muse from Murbad and all stay temporarily in Buldana. The schools would try to continue at a minimum level. The boys would stay at the farm, and the girls continue to board at the Free Methodist school.

On the Kishorganj side there were only 3 missionaries left where there had been 13. Famine, earthquake, and political upheavals had damaged all mission work. Yet the Kishorganj mission showed more gain than any other there. The Board of General Superintendents agreed to allow us a year of trial; but by the time they reached home, the depression was so bad, they sent word that the eastern Indian work must be closed and transfer what could be carried over to the western side.

On March 1, 1931, Mom and Dad waved good-bye to the Franklins and Miss Varnedoe at the Calcutta pier and went back to conclude the legal details of the property.

In the midst of closing her work at Murbad, Miss Eltie Muse took sick. The missionaries sent for an ambulance and a nurse from a hospital in Bombay. When the nurse walked into Miss Muse's room, she took one look and said, "Smallpox."

The hospital staff worked valiantly to save her, but it was the very worst type of the loathsome disease—the same kind that had taken the life of Miss Pearl Simmons years before. On March 16, 1930, she died. Four missionaries attended the quiet funeral, and they laid her away in a European cemetery in Bombay. Miss Amanda Mellies helped Mom and Dad sort Miss Muse's personal effects. When the will was probated, a fine 1929 Model A Ford had been given to Dad as superintendent to be used for mission work.

Dad was thrilled. It was his first car in India. During the 10 years he had been home, things had changed until very little missionary traveling was done in the tonga and cart. The Model A fairly flew over the district on petrol wings. Dad carried a pick, a shovel, and a boy in the back of his car as standard equipment for leveling the high crown of the road and removing rocks so that the universal joint and the differential could be spared.

School! From the beginning of his career as a missionary in 1904, Dad had dreamed of securing his own education, and with it shared his desire to provide education for Indian boys and girls. When the senior missionary assigned him to be school principal, Dad was thrilled. It was a bitter disappointment when the senior staff left abruptly and took the schoolchildren with them. It was some small comfort that a few of the children found their way back over a period of years.

It was many years before the dream of a school could be realized again. But eventually a small school for boys was again started; and as the Christian community grew, the need for a girls' school became pressing.

At first the small group of girls were taught wherever there happened to be room: a chapel, a missionary's home, or any room that could be spared, or sometimes just under a tree. They were boarded at the Free Methodist mission.

Eventually the Free Methodists asked the Nazarenes to move the girls to make room for their own. Land was found and money squeezed out of the falling General Budget[33] to purchase it. They broke ground for the building October 1930 and finished it enough for occupancy at the beginning of school in 1932.

Americans can scarcely realize what was involved in constructing a building in India. A firm of architects in Bombay made the preliminary drawings for the school, but they were 300 miles distant by train, plus 42 by car. The first thing to be done on the site was to erect temporary shelters of bamboo matting and cornstalks for the workmen and their families. Then two carts with iron water barrels had to be constructed to haul water. Dad bought a book in Bombay and from it learned how to make three reinforced concrete tanks to hold the water for building. Constructed in Buldana, the tanks were hauled 14 miles to Chikhli. Lumber was cut in the jungle, hauled in, and sawed on the grounds. Stone for the plinth was broken in the jungle, hauled to the site, trimmed by hand, and fitted in. Broken stone for road metal was chipped by hand with little mallets, packed into the foundation, and tamped on the floors. Small limestones were gathered in nearby riverbeds and fields, delivered at so much a cubic foot, fired in the kiln, mixed with sand and water, and ground into mortar by two mills constructed on the site and operated by bullock power.

---

[33] The General Budget is now called World Evangelism Fund. It is a centralized fund which supports the missions work of the Church of the Nazarene.

A fine, U-shaped building appropriate to the needs, the climate, and the country was finished. They also built a home for the missionary who would be in charge, and dug a well. Through two hot seasons Dad and Mom stayed with the building work. When in 1931 they went to Darjeeling in the rainy season, they received a jubilant telegram of three words from Rev. John McKay: "Water, water, water!"

The day of dedication was July 6, 1932. Dad and Mom, exhausted from the long months of supervision, were not there. They had gone to Ootacamund (OO-tuh-kuh-mund) for a much-needed vacation. But Dad spoke in the chapel when they returned.

It would be wonderful to say that from this time on, steady gains and great victories came to the India work. However , the disagreeable truth is that two years after the building was sacrificially completed, the school was closed. So were all the other schools, and some of the pastors had to be dismissed. The drop in the value of the dollar depleted the mission funds.

> It would be wonderful to say that from this time on, steady gains and great victories came to the India work. However, ...

These drastic measures lasted for only one year. Appeals went out, the church at home rallied, people gave sacrificially, and in July 1935, the schools reopened.

There is no individual church ever organized that does not have problems peculiar to itself. The church in Hatedi (HAW-terd- ee) had just such a problem. Our first convert, Babaji, was doing considerable colporteur work in the vicinity and holding a small group of Christians together. We had good friends there, but we also had bitter enemies. No one would rent a house in which Babaji might live. Dad bought the only suitable piece of land with a well in all Hatedi, from a man who lived in a village three miles away. It was done very quietly for fear the people would persuade the man not to sell. A few days later when Dad went to stake out the lot and make plans for erecting a house, the headman of the village and his friends came and said that the brother of the seller owned the part fronting the road. Knowing that these cases do often develop, Dad was inclined to think it might be so; but when the headman failed to produce the brother, Dad concluded it was a bluff and decided to call it. Driving the stakes and drawing a line between them, he declared that this was our land and that we would put fences on these lines. If anyone had a claim, he could present it to the court, and we would see about it there. The headman and all of the villagers were standing around. Taking his camera, Dad snapped a quick picture of them and told them that if there was trouble, he could call them all as witnesses; and they could not say they were not present, for he had the picture as proof. A murmur of dismay went over the crowd, and the "brother" never appeared. The house was built, the preacher worked faithfully in the area, and many were converted. The headman and some of his friends became warm friends of Dad in later years.

The problem of the early church in Manubai (MUN-oo-bai) was external in the beginning but later developed into internal strife.

Caste dominated everything among the Hindus in those days. While Hindus, the group who were now Christians had obtained their water from a nearby spring; but when the spring unaccountably dried up one drought season shortly after they were converted, the Christians were naturally blamed. "You say your Jesus is alive," the caste people taunted when they went to another well for water; "go and ask Him for water." And they would pour out only a little and grudgingly give it to the Christians. But the idea so sarcastically thrown at them sounded like a good one. There was a vacant space directly in front of their mud huts. It was cracked and dried by the intense heat, but the people gathered on it, knelt, and asked God in the name of Jesus to give them water. Then they began to dig a well.

Down about six feet they struck rock and appealed to the mission for blasting powder. A Hindu who understood blasting rock was sent, along with the powder, to superintend the job. Every few feet he would stop and ask that a coconut be offered to his gods. While he sat, the Christians went on digging until he would finally join them. One night, as they were gathering up their tools, the rock seemed damp. A rag was stuffed into a crack. In the morning, the rag was wet. The excited Hindu would not go down into the well until a goat was sacrificed.

As before, the Christians climbed down and began to work without him. Soon the trembling Hindu went down too. A few days more, and the well was 15 feet deep. A charge was fired, and the water gushed in so rapidly that they had to hurry to get the rest of the rubbish and the tools out. A wall was built from the rock up to the surface of the ground, proper top stones were placed, and there is no finer water in the whole village. The well is a monument to the fact that Jesus Christ lives and answers the prayer of faith. It has never dried up in the most severe drought.

It was the habit of this group of Christians to hold a prayer meeting in the center of their section of town every morning, before going to their work. It went on for a long time until one day someone got out of harmony and stirred up such a fuss in the village that nearly all of the Christians were involved. Many were ready to give up their faith. In despair a delegation came to Buldana, 30 miles away, asking Dad to come to Manubai and settle their problems for them. Dad sent the delegation back with instructions on how to settle things, but they were not ready to accept his advice. A second message was sent, saying that if he was too busy to come to them, could they come to him?

"Yes," Dad answered, "I will hear you, but you must follow these instructions.

"All who are involved in the affair must come. When you are ready to start, you must hold a prayer meeting in which all are to pray. Every three miles along the way, you must all get out of your carts and hold a meeting in which everyone is to pray. When you arrive, if you have met these conditions, I will hear your troubles and judge for you."

The Manubai Christians agreed to the terms. But they never reached Buldana. Before the first prayer meeting was over, their differences were dropped, and their wounds healed.

Most of our pastors were only a few years away from idolatry and the ideas and patterns of life that had been handed down for generations. Over the years, a feeling developed among some that the mission was favoring certain ones over others; the former caste to which each Christian had belonged played a part in the rankling undercurrent of dissatisfaction.

The missionaries were aware that there was a block of some kind to the long-prayed-for revival. The unity and fellowship so necessary between preachers of a close-knit district did not exist. But no one was prepared when, in the midst of conducting district business, thinly veiled insinuations suddenly flared into open accusations, hurled like thunderbolts from one side of the room to the other. Some were justified grievances, some were not.

Dad was presiding as district superintendent; and after the first stunning shock was over, he called for an extended recess of convention business and changed the order of the meeting. Now was the time to sweep out the closet and clear the hearts of what should not be there. All would have a chance to speak in turn for as long as they wished the floor; there was to be no repeating of anything after it had been said unless something new would be added. This would continue until there was nothing more. Asking those who could write to take notes, and instructing the secretary to set down complete minutes, Dad himself made a detailed record, and the other missionaries did the same.

For three days, the accusing went on. Each morning Dad or one of the others would give an exhortation to the assembly, pointing out that church disagreements were no new thing. The Early Christian Church had many vital differences to be settled. By the morning of the fourth day, everyone was silent. There was nothing more to be said.

Dad called a recess, stating the hour when all were to return. Then he found a piece of wire and twisted it into a large basket. The night before, while praying, Dad had received his divine inspiration. He placed the basket on the stone floor of the church before the altar.

"Everything is clean," he told them in essence. "All you have kept in your hearts is out now. It is on the paper. It is in the notes you have written down. It is in the notes I have written. The whole record is in the minutes the secretary has kept. It is all here. To those who cannot write and have no notes, here is paper for you. It represents all you have said and all you have heard in the past three days. These notes and this paper represent the years this has grown in your hearts. Here is my account. I place it before God's altar in this basket. The secretary will place the full record in here too. Now come, all of you, and let us put this evil thing into God's hands."

Solemnly, quietly, with strained faces, they marched in single file and placed their notes or their paper on the pile in the basket before the altar and went from there to stand against the walls in a circle around the church.

"We do not want this anymore," Dad half-preached, half-prayed. "We have laid it on Your altar, O God, that it might be purged from our hearts. May Thy Holy Spirit burn it out of our souls that we might be one, welded, fused, united in Thee to clear the way for revival and to spread Thy gospel."

Every eye watched Superintendent Tracy Sahib as he went to the basket and touched a match to the piled papers, then stepped back to join the circle. And as the flames licked up and up in the basket, the silence breathed and throbbed. Their accusations were going, their differences were ascending in smoke; their evil thoughts, their bitterness against one another—everything was being cleansed in the refining fire of love and unity and forgiveness, and the records were burning to black ashes, to be held against them no more.

As the last crackling flame leaped and died, the tense people, all with joined hands in an unbroken circle, sang, "Blest be the tie that binds / Our hearts in Christian love." Over and over they sang it, their faces shining with the joy and happiness of God.

As a great, heaving volcano, the deep poison was spewed out, and for the first time the Church of the Nazarene in India stood completely united, ready for a revival to be poured out on everyone.

The seeds from the years of faithful touring took hold at last. There emerged a few areas, a few groups of villages where sincere inquirers and honest seekers lived. At the turn of the year 1930-31, it seemed to Dad that the time had come to climax the touring season with a period of reaping. Word was broadcast that if the people would gather in two convenient places, Chikhli and Dhad (DHARD), there would be transportation by mission vehicles the rest of the way to Buldana to take part in the first Inquirers' Meeting ever to be held on our district—six days of intensified evangelism.

Our church and Christian congregation: Buldana, Berar, India, 1930.

The tract recounts:

We expected about 40 adults, but more than 125 came, and it taxed our transportation facilities to the limit," Dad wrote. "If you had been here, your hearts would have been greatly stirred, as ours were. There they came—men, women, and children by the carload and the truckload from villages within a radius of about 70 miles, Hindus of the lower castes all coming to a revival meeting with three of their own *sadhus*, religious leaders, among them. These were all leading people among their castes, sincere inquirers after the way of life (the preachers had weeded out the curiosity seekers). Tents were erected near the church. The Christian community took people into their homes, and two houses were rented. Many brought their grain with them for food. It was the sensation of the whole countryside.

Most of the Christians had to remain away; there was no room for them in the church.

The program was revivalistic and instructional, teaching the doctrinal and practical phases of Christianity. Mornings, the preachers and missionaries preached. In the afternoon, services were held separately for men and women, with opportunity to pray and to ask questions. The evening services were evangelistic with Mrs. May McKay as the preacher. Practically all of them went forward for prayers and prayed to the best of their ability during the meetings. Some came several times.

> **Most of the Christians had to remain away; there was no room for them in the church.**

Naturally there was opposition. Some met the people as they left the meetings and argued against what had been said. Some shouted and blew bugles outside during the services.

Twelve were baptized quietly in the church on Sunday.

The second year that the Inquirers' Meeting was held, about 125 again attended. Most of those who have attended have not worshiped idols for many years.

Chapter 10

The Voice of Rejoicing
and Salvation
Psalm 118:15

A camp meeting in the jungle! What was it? The Hindus certainly did not know. Neither did the Christians. None had ever experienced it except the missionaries. Families would need to leave their homes and employment for a few days and go off into an uninhabited place to worship God. All who wished were welcome to come, but it was to be primarily a time of refreshing for the Christians. A location was found on the lowland plain at the foot of the ghats (ghawts). It was cool and pleasant, now that the monsoon rains were ended.

A road was cut into the interior of the jungle a mile or so. Underbrush and small trees had to be cleared before a tabernacle and living shelters could be erected and tents pitched for the missionary families. The nearly dry, stony riverbed had a little trickle of water in it.

In India and other contexts where the majority of the population lives on very low income, faithfulness to the church and mission, and the sacrifices made to attend an assembly or camp meeting, has profound impact on a family's survival. To lose the little money they would earn if they stayed home and worked was real sacrifice. And yet they came to camp meeting singing. Those who had carts piled them high with dishes, grain, bedding, lanterns, and kerosene. They hitched up the bullocks, tied the family buffalo on behind to provide milk for the babies, and climbed aboard. Some rode bicycles, but most of the people walked, carrying their supplies in bundles balanced on their heads.

The total cost for the entire camp that first year was around $70.00. Those who counted said there were 451 in attendance.

The camp rules were simple. Their tiny family shelters made of woven bamboo matting must be handled carefully because the matting and poles had been rented. Stone fireplaces for cooking food were to be well out in the open, and no fire at all was allowed inside the shelter. The neighboring *jowar*[34] fields were not to be disturbed in any way. Sanitation rules must be strictly obeyed.

No series of services of this nature ends without what is known as a "break." Something happens when there is such intense prayer and travail of soul. All week some had gone out after the short afternoon service to find a tree or a rock in the jungle where they could pray alone. Others met in groups according to age. On Saturday afternoon

---

[34] *Jawar* is a grain type that is often used in making roti, a traditional Indian bread.

one by one the boys prayed through. The older boys, led by Brother Beals, broke the barrier first, asking forgiveness for meanness and fighting and lies and stealing. One by one they reached the bottom and struck fire. The smaller boys were praying through, too. Toward evening those in camp began to hear the triumphal march of victory, as 40 boys marched out of the jungle 2 by 2, singing at the top of their voices and clapping their hands. "*Yesu Masiki Jay*" (YAY-shoo MUH-SEE-kee Jay), "Victory to Jesus, the Messiah," they shouted. The answering shout that went up through the camp was deafening.

Down in the riverbed there was weeping. The older girls had not made much spiritual progress. "Will you ask that they come and pray for us?" they begged Miss Mellies. She sent word, and the army of boys turned in their direction. Surrounding the girls, the boys knelt in the sand, and the girls began to pray in earnest. At last the shout of complete victory went up, and they came marching in. It was dark and time for the evening service. No one thought of food. They marched to the tabernacle. Eighty-four had met God that one day.

The tide of evangelism did not end with the camp meeting. For the first time the Indian preachers toured on their own without a missionary accompanying them. The schoolboys formed evangelistic bands and went out every week to preach in the villages. One band took packs on their backs and walked 250 miles and preached in 40 different villages. Some of our finest preachers and their wives were boys and girls who were in that camp. So great was the impact on the entire Christian community that within five years the church membership increased more than 100 percent.

Dad's interest in the propagation of holiness was not confined to preaching, studying, and literature. Any ideas or methods used by any group, he surveyed thoroughly. "Methods that were once necessary and successful may need progressive alteration," Dad sometimes said. "And eventually missionary work, which is ultimately temporary in nature, must finally give way to group organization, the indigenous church."

This was it. This was the goal that Dad had been working toward during his entire years in India: the church, the Indian church, to be the fire-filled, Spirit-empowered organization functioning for the salvation of souls and the spreading of holiness in India.

This was it. This was the goal that Dad had been working toward during his entire years in India.

The climax came when the history-making First District Assembly was officially and eagerly organized on November 24, 1937, by General Superintendent J. B. Chapman. Six young men were ordained. And when this new baby district cast its first vote, their sound judgment and discernment were apparent, for they chose S. J. Bhujbal (BHOO-juh-buhl) as their first district superintendent—a powerful preacher, a great soul winner, and a good organizer.

Exactly 30 years to the month from the time they sailed to India for the first time, Dad and Mom boarded ship for home. Dad had been able to serve only 4 1/2 years of his third term. In the 1932 Council Meeting, while speaking in the opening session, his tongue and throat suddenly froze—he could not speak. For about a minute he stood there struggling, looking at his colleagues helplessly. Mom was up in an instant and ran to him. Brother Beals was close behind. Supporting him on each side, they forced him into a chair; then he said, "I'm all right now," and continued conducting the meeting. From that time on he could not be trusted by himself. Mom went with him almost everywhere, once sleeping in the car alone a few nights while Dad went on to another village with one of the Indian men.

The next February, 1933, a similar attack occurred, followed by a numbness in his right arm up to the armpit that lasted for 20 hours. Later his legs gave out, and he began having trouble with clogged veins. Reluctantly the Executive Committee of the council recognized the emergency and sent a request to the board in Kansas City for the Tracys' retirement.

Dad wrote his last report to the council. Following this, he stayed in bed for a time in a state of exhaustion.

"The call!" he moaned to Mom. "Sometimes through these 30 years it was all I had left, and now it seems that it, too, has gone."

But Dad was mistaken. The call had not gone; it had only moved on to another encampment. And when, a year later, he found it again, it was just as real, just as challenging as before. This time he saw it standing still over Brooklyn.

Utica Avenue Church! Mom and Dad had farewelled from it twice and been welcomed twice. And now, a year

Tracy in retirement in Brooklyn, N.Y.

after their return, the church needed a pastor and found that Dad was ready.

When tenement dwellers would not open doors to his calling, Dad resorted to the mail to reach the community. He pastored the church and served the district for six years.

But the time came when Dad's physical activities had to dwindle and then cease altogether. His heart, weakened through the years by rheumatic fever, typhoid, and bouts with malaria, began to fail. For a year and a half he continued the printing work, lying down when the attacks came. But he had to resign his church.

The attacks grew longer, then intensified, until at last paroxysmal tachycardia added itself to the four major and five minor ailments of his heart. After two short, sharp struggles he could not survive any longer. He was just 60 years old. We were all at his bedside that Monday evening, September 28, 1942. Mom and we three children, Martha's family, and Phil's family—and the doctor who lived just half a block away and had spent many hours with him keeping him alive.

Humanly speaking, it still does not seem as though Dad was expendable to the work of God's kingdom here, for trained, valuable, and faithful laborers are few. But the patriarch Daniel saw it clearly just before he laid down his stylus for the last time. There is a period of rest before the end of the days shall come, when Dad will stand beside the others in his allotted place. Rev. Paul Hill touched the same core of the great plan for us all when he said, "The resurrection day is on God s program. We shall meet again."

Dad was like an Old Testament patriarch. He laid plans for his people like a Moses, leading them ahead under the cloud and fire. He prepared the way for a new and better life like a Joseph. There were times he stood alone like a Daniel, fighting the darkness. As did Joshua, he presumed to blow the trumpet of salvation and holiness. He built the Kingdom like a David and a Solomon. And with Jeremiah and Isaiah, he literally wept for the souls of his people. He loved them more than his own life.

> **Dad was like an Old Testament patriarch.**

India is changing. Even before Dad's time there was no more suttee, where widows were forced to throw themselves on the burning pyres of their deceased husbands. The crocodiles of the Ganges have not fed on little girl babies since the turn of the century. And the heavy chains of caste have officially been dropped off. The restrictions that do not grant visas to new evangelistic foreign missionaries are a cue for the Indian church to be ready to stand alone and spread the gospel as they have received it.

There is no finis to this account of Tracy Sahib [friend] of India. The pages are turning, but the story is not ended. It will go on and on, "clearer than the noonday" (Job 11:17) as the years ahead move into the past. For the darkness has already broken into the morning of an established church in India, and this small hint of dawn ushered in by one missionary pioneer is leaping higher and higher, shining "more and more unto the perfect day" (Prov. 4:18).

Postlude: A Splendid Sacrifice

"You can't cross the sea
by standing and staring at the water."

"Let us not pray to be sheltered from dangers,
but to be fearless in facing them."
Rabindranath Tagore

The richness of Indian culture, with its complications and contrasts, is well illustrated in the dramatic writings and poetry of the Bengali poet Rabindranath Tagore. He was the first non-European to win the Nobel prize for literature in 1913. It is into this world that L. S. Tracy stepped as a 22-year-old single missionary in 1903, only five years after the first Nazarene party had come ashore to lay the initial groundwork of what they hoped would be a church.

What Tracy, and the others, faced was a world about which they had little clue. There had been no extensive cultural studies or graduate programs. In fact, Tracy had barely completed high school. All he knew was that he had a flaming passion to bring the light of Jesus' message to a place that had not heard it before. The vicissitudes of life, even of survival, were yet to be learned.

The sacrifice of health, home, and hearth were as nothing to one with vision, energy, and a calling.

Jesus instructed His disciples (Mark 4:31-32, CEB) to
"Consider a mustard seed. When
scattered on the ground, it's the smallest
of all the seeds on the earth; but when
planted, it grows and becomes the largest
of all vegetable plants."

Could Tracy and others have imagined that the tiny seeds they were planting would sprout to become what the Church of the Nazarene is today in India and South Asia? At one point, Tracy went seven years without seeing even one single convert to Christ, and then it was an elderly village woman. How many 21st-century Christians would have that kind of dogged tenacity?

Christian Protestant missions in South Asia were "organized" into geographical areas, a system called "comity." This term was adopted from agreements which had been reached between nations to promote the notion of a voluntary agreement to sustain social harmony, based on common social values and associations and to avoid the proselytizing of members of one denomination of members of another denomination. Thus, in colonial India, Methodists might work in one area, Lutherans in another, Presbyterians another. Over time Nazarenes were "given" three areas, all small in geography. In the 1930's these were consolidated into one area in central India in what became the post-Independence state of Maharashtra. Until the 1970's this system prevailed. However, as demographics shifted, and many of the children of converts move to urban areas in the country, the system broke down.

Following the disruptions of World War II and the turbulence of the movement for independence of India from British colonial rule, the missionaries knew that major changes were occurring. They recognized that demographic shifts were inevitable—that many Nazarene young people were moving away from the small rural area in which Nazarene work had existed for a number of years. This included some pastors, who began work here and there on an independent basis. As early as 1947 some missionaries were "assigned" to open work in Bombay, but these efforts came to naught because of the extreme high costs involved and the limited resources for mission work during that period of time.

One of these efforts which bore fruit was the opening of a small work in the city of Aurangabad, located some 150 miles northeast of Bombay, by pastor Luther Manmothe. This occurred in 1962. It is a church that stabilized and grew into a significant district center in the state of Maharashtra.

In 1974 Rev. and Mrs. Bronell Greer were sent to open work in or around Bombay (Mumbai) and from there shifted to southern India, settling in the area around Bangalore.[35]

---

[35] Officially, the physical move of Rev. and Mrs. Bronell Greer to western Maharashtra and later to southern India, as referenced above, is considered the "breakout" that set the Nazarene denomination on a new and expanded course in South Asia. Nobody, not even the missionaries of great vision, could have foreseen the "explosion" of growth which was to occur beginning in the 1990's and continuing to this day.

Shortly afterward, Rev. and Mrs. John Anderson were asked to open work in northern India in the capital city of Delhi. In the 1990's, having succeeded in starting work in northern India, they were reassigned to eastern India to open work in Calcutta (Kolkata). Now Nazarenes had work in every quadrant of India: north, south, east, west, and central.

This does not mean that the work was large or easy. In fact, it was pioneering—-dealing with vast changes in a nation newly freed from the colonial rule of Britain, with a population of increasing life span, educational opportunity, population, and wealth. There were legal issues to settle, a strategy to develop, properties to purchase and manage, theological clarity to maintain, new dynamics which effected such issues as ministerial education, compassionate ministries, discipleship, and definitions of what was to constitute a true indigenous church in a very complicated environment.

Along with this were government decrees disallowing new missionaries from abroad to enter the country permanently, which automatically thrust on Indian leaders the responsibility for the expansion of the church. In this regard, one can say that the government enhanced in many ways the development of the indigenous church by reducing its reliance on foreign funds or personnel.

Tracy (and others) could not possibly have foreseen these developments. Yet it is on their work that the stones of permanence were built. Their message, and example, endured. They were hindered neither by culture nor lack of resources, by death or ill health. God had called them. The church had commissioned them. This was their life's work.

Today's statistics are, by any calculation, impressive. That one district organized in 1938 by General Superintendent J. B. Chapman has grown now to 15 districts covering the whole of post-partition India. If you add Pakistan and Bangladesh (part of the pre-partition India) to the statistics, you can count 19 or more districts.

On those districts are 7,464 local churches, of which 3,335 are in today's India. The current membership totals are 139,087 in India, and an added 135,118 in Bangladesh and Pakistan, for a total of 274,205.

What was one Bible College teaching a few rural young men in one language, went through significant, and at times, uncomfortable change in the late 1990's. Sometimes, decisions are made without a full grasp of their potential outcomes. It was clear that something had to change, to bring Nazarene Bible College of India into a more effective role as the education provider for India and South Asia. As the church grew, it could not continue to be a small, campus-based school. In an informal conversation around a glass-topped coffee table, in the lounge of a Calcutta (now Kolkata) hotel, when I was Regional Director, I hit the table with a firm gesture that caused a brass vase to jump off the glass, and then clang back to the surface. Every eye was wide open, those present shocked that he would be so emphatic. The decision was taken to move the Bible College into a transition stage, and totally rethink the curriculum, faculty development, and delivery systems to better serve the growing fields. That decision changed the college forever. Sometimes in missions history, unplanned and unexpected decisions are taken that yield unexpected results. Today, South Asia Nazarene Bible College has 155 learning centres teaching in 19 major languages (working on facilitating five more languages in the near future), and with a total enrollment of 2,392. The first graduation ceremony of this new decentralized college saw 66 graduate, more than had been graduated from all the previous years of the college's history. God has been doing amazing things through South Asia Nazarene Bible College. Others are looking closely at the model of decentralized education that focuses on faculty development, student development and institutional development for the

Today, many local Indian Churches of the Nazarene are raising funds and sponsoring missionaries within the borders of their own lands.

purpose of preparing larger numbers of men and women for ministry and mission through the Church of the Nazarene.

But this is not just a numbers game. The influence of Christ's message is felt through a wide range of programs dealing with social issues, health care, nutrition, literacy, education, micro-enterprise, compassionate ministries, literature development, and fraternal relationships with many other Christian organizations and ministries.

Indeed, the parable of the mustard seed as taught by Jesus can be proven again and again. The challenges of today are as great, or perhaps greater, than in Tracy's day. Every new community entered, every new language or tribal group approached is a repeat of the pioneering principles this early missionaries exhibited. Today, many local Indian Churches of the Nazarene are raising funds and sponsoring missionaries within the borders of their own lands. "The gates of hell shall not prevail" is a daily living truth.

The splendid sacrifice of a life well lived does, in the end, have its own rewards.

—R. FRANKLIN COOK

A Growing Church

Editor's Note: Though some statistics have been updated within the text of this revised edition, it may prove useful to include here the latest statistics associated with India and what would have been the areas included before the partitioning of 1947.

Population

In 1947, the British Raj, Britain's Indian Empire, was partitioned into what ultimately became three countries: India, Pakistan, and Bangladesh.

"The population of undivided India in 1947 was approximately 390 million. After partition, there were 330 million people in India, 30 million in West Pakistan, and 30 million people in East Pakistan (now Bangladesh)." [36]

In July 2017, *The World Factbook*[37] lists the populations of the world areas as follows:

India	1,281,935,911
Pakistan	204,924,861
Bangladesh	157,826,578
Total	1,644,687,350

[36] Dhruv Kharabanda. "Case for acceptance of refugees into European Nations": Page 4. www.kharabanda.in/3.pdf.

[37] *The World Factbook* 2018. Washington, DC: Central Intelligence Agency, 2018. https://www.cia.gov/library/publications/resources/the-world-factbook. Information gathered from the Bangladesh, India, and Pakistan pages.

The latest available statistics of the Church of the Nazarene from 2017 are, by any calculation, impressive. That one district organized in 1938 by General Superintendent J. B. Chapman are now 15 districts covering the whole of post-partition India. If you add Pakistan and Bangladesh (part of the pre-partition India) to the statistics, you can count 19 (or more) districts.

On those districts are 7,464 local churches, of which 3,335 are in today's India. The current membership totals are 139,087 in India and an added 135,118 in Bangladesh and Pakistan for a total of 274,205.

What was one Bible College teaching a few rural young men in one language, is today a Bible College with 155 extension centers teaching in 19 major languages (working on facilitating 5 more languages in the coming years) and with a total enrollment of 2,392.

In June 1938, Reynolds Memorial Hospital was established. The hospital and its affiliated clinics in Washim, India, is a 150-bed general hospital. It serves the community and surrounding area.

Founded in 1958, the Nazarene Nurses Training College (NNTC) is situated on the Reynolds Memorial Hospital campus premises. NNTC is a recognized Christian learning Institution that aims to prepare its students for the future by emphasizing the development of fundamental nursing concepts and the application of skills, equipping students to become qualified nurses, not only in India but throughout the world.

The 2017 enrollment of NNTC was 245.

Comparative Statistics

	1947 (date of partitioning)	2017 (current)
Districts		
India	1	15
Pakistan		1
Bangladesh		3
Total Districts	1	**19**
Churches		
India		3,335
Pakistan		426
Bangladesh		3,703
Total Churches		**7,664**
Membership		
India	2,830	139,087
Pakistan		19,370
Bangladesh		115,748
Total Membership	**2,830**	**274,205**

ACT ON IT

1. L. S. Tracy and his colleagues encountered the Indian culture of his day in their efforts to bring the message of Jesus to those who had not heard. Can you identify some of the cultural issues that you face in your community, and how they impact or influence ways in which the church carries forward its mission in the world of today?

2. Check the internet for the meaning of the word "colonialism" or "colonial." In Tracy's day missionaries in India, and elsewhere, were working in a colonial environment. Note some of the ways in which the colonial environment affected the work of the newly planted church in India. Note any similarities in the current environment that could impact missions today.

3. You will notice in the text that when everything else is done and said, Tracy often came back to his central mission and calling, which was to bring the message of Jesus and salvation to people who had never heard it. In the world of today, how can, or should, we focus on our central mission and calling as Christians to bring that message to an increasingly secular environment?

4. Consider, and discuss with others, some practical ways in which the church can be, and remain, current and relevant to a changing society with differing standards and expectations?

5. Missionaries of Tracy's day were always concerned about the "next generation," and they were attempting to find ways to keep the calling of God a vibrant reality or possibility for young people. Consider, and discuss with others, how in today's church the calling of God can best be understood and applied in the life of "the next generation."

6. The place of God's Word was always important in driving the mission of the church. Identify and review what to you are key verses that should be known and understood today and how they apply to a generation consumed with internet and media formats, such as Instagram and Snapchat.

7. Pray for the work of the Church of the Nazarene in India and South Asia, which is often faced with opposition and threat of theological drift.

8. Traits we see in Tracy that kept him focused and determined in his mission were: faithful pursuit of God's will, honest and courageous dealings with both church and society, tireless effort to win the lost and establish the church, and commitment to leave India better than he found it. Do you possess such traits? How might you use these traits to strengthen your local church and community?